D1540726

THE GREAT TARIFF DEBATE, 1820-1830

Problems in American Civilization

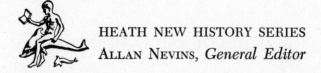

HEATH NEW HISTORY SERIES

ALLAN NEVINS, *General Editor*

THE GREAT TARIFF
DEBATE, 1820–1830

EDITED WITH AN INTRODUCTION BY

George Rogers Taylor

Problems in American Civilization

READINGS SELECTED BY THE
DEPARTMENT OF AMERICAN STUDIES
AMHERST COLLEGE

D. C. HEATH AND COMPANY: Boston

Copyright 1953 by D. C. Heath and Company

*No part of the material covered by this copyright may be reproduced
in any form without written permission of the publisher.* (5 K 2)

PRINTED IN THE UNITED STATES OF AMERICA

Offices

Boston   New York   Chicago   Dallas

Atlanta   San Francisco   London

INTRODUCTION

"Next to currency problems no purely economic subject has aroused so much interest in the United States, and played so great a part in political discussion both in and out of Congress as the tariff policy of the federal government. From the first measure to raise a revenue from import duties in 1789 until the present time no generation of the American people has escaped the tariff controversy."[1] These words of Guy S. Callender are perhaps not quite as true today as when he wrote them forty-four years ago, yet problems of international trade restriction continue to be political issues of major importance. In recent times hardly a year has gone by without a congressional battle over the reciprocal trade agreement acts and the struggle grows increasingly serious as crucial issues of domestic and foreign policy become involved. Thus those who for military and strategic reasons wish to restore the health of the Japanese economy urge the United States to lower, or at least not to raise, trade barriers against Japanese imports. On the other hand, American business and labor groups affected by Japanese competition clamor for increased protection.

Though conditions have changed in many respects since the initial major struggle over the protective tariff took place in this country in the decades following the War of 1812, there is much to

[1] Guy Stevens Callender, *Selections from the Economic History of the United States, 1765–1860* (Boston: Ginn and Co., 1909), p. 487.

be learned from a study of that controversy. This is especially true of the Tariff of 1824. Before that time sectional divisions on the issue had not yet hardened; even John C. Calhoun had favored the Tariff of 1816. But the impact of the depression of 1819–1820, the rising manufacturing industries of New England and the Middle States, and the rapid commitment of the South to cotton growing had by 1824 led to a clarification of interests and viewpoints. These views were now carefully formulated by the great sectional leaders of the period and given expression in public debates and speeches which remain to this day a storehouse of arguments for speakers on both sides of the question. It is true that bitter debates on this issue continued from time to time, for the tariff has remained a constantly recurring national problem. But most of the issues were clearly spotlighted in 1824. Moreover, at this time they were somewhat less complicated by political intrigue as in 1828 or by nullification as in the early 1830's. This, added to the caliber of the participants in the debate of 1824, has led to the focusing of this volume on the 1820's, with special attention to the Tariff of 1824.

The leading contention of the early protectionists was, as in the arguments for the Hawley-Smoot Tariff Act of 1930, that protection would alleviate the depression in agriculture and industry. And most of the other standard arguments such as that for the home market, aid to

337.9735 T214 27882 4-2-59 1.00

infant industry, and unfair dumping of foreign goods on our shores were also used to full advantage. The opposition then contended, as it has in a score of subsequent controversies, that under free trade the efficient and advantageous industries would survive, that free international trade would benefit all, and that protection was merely a device for aiding particular industries or sections of the country by levying tribute on others. None of these positions was entirely new in the 1820's but each was defended with freshness and eager conviction by able political leaders, men like Clay, Webster, and McDuffie, men whose speeches are still worth reading. A study of their logic or lack of logic, their insights and rationalizations, their broad visions and their myopias helps clarify the tariff controversies of today and tomorrow.

The readings in this volume begin with a brief summary of tariff history from 1789 to 1861 by the editor. This sketch is designed to place the controversy of the twenties in the larger setting of early tariff history. Next, extracts are presented in chronological order from the celebrated debate in the House of Representatives on the Tariff Act of 1824. The protective tariff was, of course, an essential part of Henry Clay's American system; his oration in the Eighteenth Congress set the keynote for the protectionists' speeches. Further illustration of protectionist thinking is given in the statements by John Tod of Pennsylvania, who was chairman of the House Committee on Manufactures, and by two other ardent followers of Clay, Andrew Stewart of Pennsylvania and George Holcombe of New York. The opposition to protection by the maritime and commercial interests of the North is set forth in excerpts from the speeches of Daniel Webster of Massachusetts and Samuel A. Foot of Connecti-

cut. The position of the Southern plantation interests is ably expounded in the speeches of George McDuffie of South Carolina. In order better to present this Southern viewpoint, there is included not only a considerable part of McDuffie's speech in 1824 but also an excerpt from his remarks made in 1830.

Any adequate survey of the protective controversy must take account of the enormous amount of attention it received from the press. The leading editor-publisher on the protectionist side was Hezekiah Niles of Baltimore. The editorial from his *Weekly Register,* which appears in this volume, is representative of the life-long crusade for higher duties which he carried on in the pages of this influential periodical. Ablest of the free trade journalists was Condy Raguet. His journal was first called the *Free Trade Advocate* and later the *Banner of the Constitution* (1829–1832). Though his periodicals failed through lack of popular support, the superior quality of his writing was widely recognized. A satirical article from his pen is included in this volume. It set a style upon which the better known French advocate of free trade, Frédéric Bastiat, may well have modeled his ironic essays.

A popular method at the time for the expression of public opinion was the memorial. The two here included express the economic arguments which had become basic to the two contending groups.

The classical economists, especially Adam Smith and Jean Baptiste Say, were frequently brought into the tariff debate, condemned as impractical theorists by the protectionists and cited as profound thinkers by the free traders. How much they were actually read or really influenced thought on the subject is open to question. Commenting sarcastically on references to these authors in congressional debates, John Randolph remarked, "I too, am versed *in title pages.*" In any case, a rising school of American economists entered the fray on both sides of the issue. Ablest and most original on the protectionists' side was Daniel Raymond of Baltimore. In his book, *Thoughts on Political Economy,* the first systematic text on economics to be published in this country, he violently opposed the free trade teachings of Adam Smith. The excerpt from Raymond's book which appears in this volume well illustrates the attitude of the so-called Nationalist school of American economists. Typical of free trade thought is the reading included from *Lectures on the Restrictive System* by Thomas Roderick Dew, a professor at William and Mary.

The volume is concluded by two selections from authors writing toward the end of the nineteenth century who survey the early tariff controversy from opposite viewpoints. The first, written by D. G. Harriman, at one time a Congressman from New York, presents the typical protectionist interpretation of our tariff history. The second provides an analysis by F. W. Taussig, late professor of economics at Harvard University and a specialist in international trade.

The emphasis in this volume has been deliberately placed on the economic aspects of the controversy. It would not be possible within the limits of this book of readings to include an adequate consideration of the political and constitutional aspects of the problem. Moreover, though politics, alas, is ever a real factor in molding tariff acts, it is essentially the question of the economic merits of protection which remains unresolved in popular thinking and which presents the student with a difficult puzzle. This volume presents him with the problem: How would or should he have voted on the Tariff Bill of 1824? And in the light of history and present-day facts, what position should he now take on the still controversial issues of the role of the government in regulating foreign trade?

CONTENTS

THE CLASH OF ISSUES

In Congress:

Defending The Tariff Act of 1824, Henry Clay declaimed:

". . . the bill may be postponed, thwarted, defeated. But the cause is the cause of the country, and it must and will prevail. It is founded in the interests and affections of the people. It is as native as the granite deeply embosomed in our mountains. And, in conclusion, I would pray God, in His infinite mercy, to avert from our country the evils which are impending over it, and, by enlightening our councils, to conduct us into that path which leads to riches, to greatness, to glory."

And attacking the bill, George McDuffie replied:

"And, sir, let it be remembered that a revenue system, grossly and palpably unequal in itself — a system which, under the most favorable modification, would levy the entire amount of the federal taxes from one-fifth part of the productions of the Union, while the other four-fifths are entirely exempted from all manner of imposition — let it be remembered, I say, that this is the substratum upon which has been reared this monstrous and iniquitous superstructure — the protecting system. . . .

"Let me, then, beseech the advocates of that system, in the name of our common ancestors, whose blood was mingled together as a common offering at the shrine of our common liberty — let me beseech them, by all the endearing recollections of our common history, and by every consideration that gives value to the liberty and union of these States, to retrace their steps as speedily as possible, and relieve a high-minded and patriotic people from an unconstitutional and oppressive burden, which they cannot longer bear."

Among the Economists:

Daniel Raymond (1820) reasoned this way:

"A measure of government may interfere with the private interests of an individual, or a class of individuals; but if at the same time, it promotes in a greater degree, the interests of a larger class of individuals, it will be beneficial to the nation, and will promote national wealth. . . .

"National wealth, is the effect of national industry. If you would increase the effect, you must add new force and power to the cause. A most effectual method to do this, is to give to national industry a monopoly of the home market."

But Thomas R. Dew (1829) saw the problem in a different light:

"This, then, is the great principle which will ever ensure the proper application of labour and capital. The vigilant eye of government is not required to watch over any of the departments of industry. Man is governed by his interests. His interest will generally prompt him into that employment, where all the advantages taken together are greatest; or in other words, that employment which is the most profitable to him. And that will, generally speaking, be the most profitable, whose products are not in sufficient abundance for the demand.

"It is thus clear, that every individual will prosper most, when his exertions are properly directed by an enlightened self-interest, guided by the principle just stated; and that the wants of society, so far as they can be supplied, will be effectually supplied in this manner. . . .

"Where then, let me ask, is the need for the interference of government? It must be a blind director. It cannot produce a better employment of the labour and capital of an individual, than he or his friends can choose."

And the verdict of History?

President William McKinley writing in 1896 concluded:

"The effects of this legislation [The Tariff Act of 1824] were immediate and gratifying, realizing the predictions of its friends and promoters. Every class felt the revival of business and the general prosperity; the factory, the farm, our shipping, mercantile, commercial, and mining interests all enjoyed the change."

But writing in 1909, the economic historian Guy S. Callender concludes:

"It is not going too far to say that no important feature in our economic development during that period [i.e. 1789–1860] can be attributed unmistakably to tariff legislation. No important industries can be said to have been created or prevented from growth by that legislation. Other influences determined the main features of development, and the tariff policy did nothing more than modify them a little, where it had any effect at all."

I HISTORICAL SUMMARY

George Rogers Taylor: THE PROTECTIVE TARIFF, 1789–1860

THE nature and the height of the duties imposed on imports by the federal government were determined by two objectives: revenue and protection to home industries. Though not always mutually exclusive, these two purposes were at least so ill-mated as to lead to almost constant difficulties in drawing up tariff measures and to cause a great deal of confused thinking. One aspect of this problem can hardly be treated without some attention to the other, but the interest here is in the tariff as an interventionist device, a method by which the state attempted to extend its help or "protection" to selected parts of the economy.

A protective element had been present in the very first tariff act, that of 1789, but Hamilton's ambitious protective system had not been adopted by Congress. Until the War of 1812 rates remained relatively low, less than 20 per cent on the value of dutiable products, and revenue consideration clearly overshadowed the protective features. In July, 1812, as a war revenue measure, Congress doubled the duties on imports for the duration of the war and for one year thereafter. By 1816 the federal treasury was overflowing with revenue, and duties might well have been returned to the prewar level. But protectionist sentiment intervened, proving sufficiently strong to make the act of 1816 mildly protectionist. The new rates,

though generally less than those prevailing during the war, were higher than the previous peacetime levels. But they were still very low as compared to some later acts. The law provided for a general level of rates on dutiable goods of about 20 per cent. Cotton and woolen cloth were to pay a duty of 25 per cent; this was to be reduced after three years to 20 per cent. Moreover, all cotton cloth was to be valued (for purposes of assessing the duty), at no less than 25 cents a square yard. This last provision was designed to keep out the cheap cottons of the Far East, but in actual practice it also proved extremely effective against English cottons when prices fell drastically in 1819. A special tariff act in 1818 repealed the provision in the earlier law that the rate on cotton and woolen textiles should be reduced to 20 per cent after three years, and substantially increased the duty on pig and bar iron and iron manufactures.

Less a party measure than later tariffs, the mildly protective act of 1816 aroused no strong opposition and actually found considerable support in the South. Even John C. Calhoun, then in his nationalist phase, was among those voting for it. But such general agreement on tariff legislation soon disappeared. The continued flood of manufactured imports in 1817 and 1818 and then the severe depression of 1819–1820 brought an aggressive and

Reprinted from George Rogers Taylor, *The Transportation Revolution, 1815–1860* (New York: Rinehart & Company, 1951), pp. 360–365, with minor revisions. Used by permission of the publishers.

persistent clamor for greatly increased duties on manufactured goods. Centered in Pennsylvania, this sentiment was also strong in all the Middle Atlantic states, southern New England, Ohio, and Kentucky. In this area great numbers of small manufacturing businesses had sprung up during the years of trade restrictions, 1808–1809 and 1812–1814. The European importations and the sharp price declines of 1819–1820 bankrupted many of these ventures and seemed to many manufacturers to present difficulties which could be overcome only if the federal government promptly adopted protective legislation.

If this depression-born enthusiasm for protection had been confined merely to the owners of manufacturing ventures, the political pressures for high import duties might not have been successful. But, fortunately for the protectionists, they now easily recruited enthuiastic support from farmers, workers, and printers. American farmers were bitterly resentful of declining prices. In March, 1817, farm crops in Pennsylvania had reached their highest monthly levels between the Revolution and the Civil War; by 1821 they had fallen by more than 50 per cent. Grain farmers were especially affected. For the whole period 1784 through 1861 the index of grain prices reached its highest annual average in 1816, its lowest in 1821. Wheat and wheat flour, the most important cash crop in such states as Pennsylvania and Maryland, suffered especially. Philadelphia superfine flour, which brought more than $14 a barrel in the spring of 1817, had fallen to $4 and even less four years later. The high prices were in large part the result of short crops in Europe which led to tremendous exports; the price decline coincided with the almost complete cessation of such exports

after 1818. With prices so low that it hardly paid farmers to haul wheat to the mill, and with little prospect of a revival of the European demand, the wheat growers of Pennsylvania, Maryland, Connecticut, and Ohio were easily persuaded that their only hope lay in enlarging the home market by protection to domestic manufacturing. In addition, other farmers, like the hemp growers of Kentucky and the sheep raisers of Ohio, Pennsylvania, and Vermont, ascribed their depression hardships to foreign imports of hemp and wool and sought a remedy in higher duties.

Also from an entirely new group, the workers in manufacturing, or mechanics as they were called, came strong support for protection. The depression of 1819–1820 produced for the first time the phenomenon in America of industrial unemployment, of workers discharged from manufacturing employment and dependent upon charity for subsistence. The number of unemployed in Philadelphia in 1819 was estimated at from 7,288 to 20,000 out of a total population of about 110,000. Similarly, in the western manufacturing center of Pittsburgh, employment in 1819 had fallen to one third of the total employed in 1815. Many of the unemployed had been workers in textile mills and iron works; others were unemployed mechanics in small shops where their interests were closely identified with those of the master workmen or manufacturers. In their distress the workmen, like their masters, blamed their condition on foreign competition and demanded increased duties. The Philadelphia shoemakers became so converted to the protectionist viewpoint that they naively carried their argument to its logical conclusion, declared New Englanders "a species of foreigners," and requested the governor and the legislature of Pennsylvania to prohibit the sale of New England shoes in Pennsylvania.[1]

Finally, the protectionist cause now received invaluable support from able writers and publicists. The free trade teachings of Adam Smith and J. B. Say, which had greatly influenced the leaders of American thought, were for the first time effectively challenged by American writers of systematic texts on political economy. Most important of these was Daniel Raymond, whose *Thoughts on Political Economy* attacked the whole Smithian system and defended protective duties as a cure for unemployment. Greatly influenced by his observation of conditions during the depression of 1819–1820, he presented a strong protectionist and nationalist viewpoint which was soon adopted by other able writers, men such as Willard Phillips, Friedrich List, and, somewhat later, Henry C. Carey. Even more influential were two publicists, those indefatigable workers in the protectionist vineyard, Hezekiah Niles and Mathew Carey. *Niles' Weekly Register,* issued from Baltimore, reached a national audience with the gospel of protection to native industries. Few publications circulated more widely, were more often quoted by other papers, or were more generally respected. Also, the successful Philadelphia printer and pamphleteer, Mathew Carey, worked and wrote tirelessly for the cause. Neither was a great thinker or system builder, but both lost no opportunity to reiterate the doctrine that prosperity, employment, and national strength depended upon prosperous native manufactures, which in turn could

[1] *United States Gazette* (April 25, 1818), cited in Malcolm Rogers Eiselen, *The Rise of Pennsylvania Protectionism* (Philadelphia: Published by the author, 1932), p. 53.

not succeed without proper protective duties.

Massachusetts was not at first one of the states clamoring for an upward revision of the tariff of 1816. The usual explanation for this emphasizes the fact that commercial interests partial to free trade continued relatively strong in the state until after 1824, when manufacturing became relatively more important and the majority of Massachusetts votes in Congress shifted over to the protectionist side. Although this was part of the picture it should not be permitted to obscure the fact that the representatives of cotton textile factories of Massachusetts were not especially active in urging higher tariffs in 1820 and 1824 because the Boston Associates, who were busily developing the Waltham system, were doing very well. In the first place, their influence had secured relatively high protection in the tariff act of 1816 under the minimum valuation clause for imported textiles; and, in the second place, their improved methods and general efficiency permitted them to continue profitable production right through the depression of 1819–1821.

The position of the South was overwhelmingly anti-tariff after 1816. Dependence of that area on foreign markets for disposal of its cotton and tobacco and the failure of the South to develop manufacturing on a considerable scale convinced southern leaders that the protective system hurt their foreign markets and increased the prices they had to pay for manufactured goods.

The rising tide of protectionist sentiment led to an attempt to pass an act appreciably increasing the tariff in 1820. This bill passed the House and failed by only one vote in the Senate, but a similar measure won easily in 1824. Rates on important manufactures as well as on the products of the farms, mines, and quarries were solidly increased by this act and then given a further boost in 1828 when, with the passage of the so-called Tariff of Abominations, rates reached their highest general level before the Civil War. This latter measure, the result of political maneuvering, was especially distasteful to New England representatives. At the same time that they voted for high duties on textiles, they were forced also to approve rates which penalized wool manufacturers by high duties on raw wool, shipbuilders by high duties on hemp and ship iron, and rum manufacturers by a high tariff on molasses. Special tariff acts in 1830 and a general revision in 1832 modified the provisions of the law of 1828 most objectionable to New England manufacturers by reducing rates on needed imported materials. They also helped temporarily to reduce redundant Treasury receipts by placing such commodities as sugar, tea, and coffee on the free list.

Though the tariff of 1832 had reduced rates to a level about equal to that of the tariff of 1824, it was definitely and systematically protective in intent. The act was bitterly resisted by the Southerners because it seemed definitely to fasten the protective system upon the country. Leading the opposition, South Carolina called a state convention which declared the tariff acts of 1828 and 1832 nullified after February 1, 1833. President Jackson replied with his famous toast, "Our Federal Union — it must be preserved!" The crisis passed with the adoption of the Compromise Tariff of 1833. This measure provided that by July 1, 1842, duties should be lowered to 20 per cent, a level close to the average duties imposed under the tariff of 1816. This reduction was to be made in steps, one tenth in each of the years 1834, 1836, 1838, and 1840, and six tenths in 1842, of which one half was to

come on January 1 and the rest on July 1.

Though these reductions were made as planned, the low level finally reached by the middle of 1842 was not permitted to prevail for more than a few weeks. The strongly protectionist Whig party had gained control of the government, the deep depression beginning in 1839 had led to a popular demand for remedial legislation, and temporary Treasury deficits seemed to indicate a need for higher duties. On August 30, 1842, a new tariff act went into effect which substantially raised duties. But in 1844 the Democrats returned to power, business improved, and Treasury surpluses reappeared. Over strong opposition from New England and the Middle Atlantic states, the so-called Walker Tariff was adopted in 1846. Though still mildly protective, this act brought a general lowering of rates. It also greatly simplified the form of tariff legislation by classifying all dutiable commodities in a small number of groups or schedules and provided for single ad valorem rates on each schedule.

There followed a decade during which protective sentiment was at low ebb. Times were generally good and Treasury receipts more than ample. In line with growing free-trade sentiment and in order to reduce redundant funds in the Treasury, the tariff act of 1857 was passed to lower duties still further. The free list was enlarged in this tariff, and rates now averaged less than 20 per cent. In harmony with European trends, the United States appeared to be moving toward a policy of genuine free trade.

The panic of 1857 broke in August. The Treasury ran sizable deficits and had to resort to borrowing to meet current obligations. Manufacturing interests in New England and New York (especially the manufacturers of woolens, who benefited from lowered rates on imports of raw wool) seem to have been fairly well satisfied with the tariff of 1857. But not so the iron and steel interests of Pennsylvania or the sheep raisers of Ohio and Vermont. The rising Republican party, making a high protective tariff one of the chief planks in its platform, won the election of 1860. In 1861, after some of the southern members had withdrawn, Congress passed the Morrill Tariff for the twin purposes of increased revenue and higher protection.

II   THE DEBATE IN CONGRESS

Henry Clay of Kentucky, Speaker of the House of Representatives

IN casting our eyes around us, the most prominent circumstance which fixes our attention, and challenges our deepest regret, is, the general distress which pervades the whole country. It is forced upon us by numerous facts of the most incontestable character. It is indicated by the diminished exports of native produce; by the depressed and reduced state of our foreign navigation; by our diminished commerce; by successive unthreshed crops of grain, perishing in our barns and barn-yards for the want of a market; by the alarming diminution of the circulation medium; by the numerous bankruptcies, not limited to the trading classes, but extending to all orders of society; by an universal complaint of the want of employment, and a consequent reduction of the wages of labor; by the ravenous pursuit after public situations, not for the sake of their honors, and the performance of their public duties, but as a means of private subsistence; by the reluctant resort to the perilous use of paper money; by the intervention of legislation in the delicate relation between debtor and creditor; and, above all, by the low and depressed state of the value of almost every description of the whole mass of the property of the nation, which has, on an average, sunk not less than about fifty per cent. within a few years. This distress pervades every part of the Union, every class of society; all feel it, though it may be felt, at different places, in different degrees. It is like the atmosphere which surrounds us — all must inhale it, and none can escape it. In some places, it has burst upon our people without a single mitigating circumstance to temper its severity. In others, more fortunate, slight alleviations have been experienced, in the expenditure of the public revenue, and in other favoring causes. A few years ago, the planting interest consoled itself with its happy exemption; but it has now reached this interest also, which experiences, though with less severity, the general suffering. It is most painful to me to

With the exception of the final speech by George McDuffie of South Carolina, the following debates in Congress are taken from the *Annals of Congress*, 18 Congress, 1 session (Washington: Gales and Seaton, 1856). Mr. Clay's speech appears on pages 1962–2001 for March 31, 1824.

attempt to sketch or to dwell on the gloom of this picture. But I have exaggerated nothing. Perfect fidelity to the original would have authorized me to have thrown on deeper and darker hues. And it is the duty of the statesman, no less than that of the physician, to survey, with a penetrating, steady, and undismayed eye, the actual condition of the subject on which he would operate; to probe to the bottom the diseases of the body politic, if he would apply efficacious remedies. We have not, thank God, suffered in any great degree for food. But distress, resulting from the absence of a supply of the mere physical wants of our nature, is not the only, nor, perhaps, the keenest distress, to which we may be exposed. Moral and pecuniary suffering is, if possible, more poignant. It plunges its victim into hopeless despair. It poisons, it paralyzes, the spring and source of all useful exertion. Its unsparing action is collateral as well as direct. It falls with inexorable force, at the same time, upon the wretched family of embarrassment and insolvency, and upon its head. They are a faithful mirror, reflecting back upon him, at once, his own frightful image, and that, no less appalling, of the dearest objects of his affection. What is the *cause* of this wide-spreading distress, of this deep depression, which we behold stamped on the public countenance? We are the same people. We have the same country. We cannot arraign the bounty of Providence. The showers still fall in the same grateful abundance. The sun still casts his genial and vivifying influence upon the land; and the land, fertile and diversified in its soils as ever, yields to the industrious cultivator, in boundless profusion, its accustomed fruits, its richest treasures. Our vigor is unimpaired. Our industry has not relaxed. If ever the accusation of wasteful extravagance could be made against our

people, it cannot now be justly preferred. They, on the contrary, for the few last years at least, have been practising the most rigid economy. The causes, then, of our present affliction, whatever they may be, are human causes, and human causes not chargeable upon the people, in their private and individual relations.

What, again I would ask, is the cause of the unhappy condition of our country, which I have faintly depicted? It is to be found in the fact that, during almost the whole existence of this Government, we have shaped our industry, our navigation, and our commerce, in reference to an extraordinary war in Europe, and to foreign markets, which no longer exist; in the fact that we have depended too much upon foreign sources of supply, and excited too little the native; in the fact that, whilst we have cultivated, with assiduous care, our foreign resources, we have suffered those at home to wither, in a state of neglect and abandonment. The consequence of the termination of the war of Europe has been the resumption of European commerce, European navigation, and the extension of European agriculture and European industry, in all its branches. Europe, therefore, has no longer occasion to any thing like the same extent as that which she had during her wars, for American commerce, American navigation, the produce of American industry. Europe in commotion, and convulsed throughout all her members, is to America no longer the same Europe as she is now, tranquil, and watching with the most vigilant attention all her own peculiar interests, without regard to the operation of her policy upon us. The effect of this altered state of Europe upon us has been to circumscribe the employment of our marine, and greatly to reduce the value of the produce of our territorial labor. . . .

The greatest want of civilized society is a market for the sale and exchange of the surplus of the produce of the labor of its members. This market may exist at home or abroad, or both, but it must exist somewhere, if society prospers, and wherever it does exist, it should be competent to the absorption of the entire surplus of production. It is most desirable that there should be both a home and a foreign market. But, with respect to their relative superiority, I cannot entertain a doubt. The home market is first in order, and paramount in importance. The object of the bill under consideration is to create this home market, and to lay the foundations of a genuine American policy. It is opposed; and it is incumbent upon the partisans of the foreign policy (terms which I shall use without any invidious intent) to demonstrate that the foreign market is an adequate vent for the surplus produce of our labor. But is it so? 1. Foreign nations cannot, if they would, take our surplus produce. If the source of supply, no matter of what, increases in a greater ratio than the demand for that supply, a glut of the market is inevitable, even if we suppose both to remain perfectly unobstructed. The duplication of our population takes place in terms of about twenty-five years. The term will be more and more extended as our numbers multiply. But it will be a sufficient approximation to assume this ratio for the present. We increase, therefore, in population at the rate of about four per cent. per annum. Supposing the increase of our production to be in the same ratio, we should, every succeeding year, have, of surplus produce, four per cent. more than that of the preceding year, without taking into the account the differences of seasons which neutralize each other. If, therefore, we are to rely upon the foreign market exclusively, foreign consumption ought to be shown to be increasing in the same ratio of four per cent. per annum, if it be an adequate vent for our surplus produce. But, as I have supposed the measure of our increasing production to be furnished by that of our increasing population; so the measure of their power of consumption must be determined by that of the increase of their population. Now, the total foreign population, who consume our surplus produce, upon an average, do not double their aggregate number in a shorter term than that of about one hundred years. Our powers of production increase then in a ratio four times greater than their powers of consumption. And hence their utter inability to receive from us our surplus produce.

But, secondly; if they could, they will not. The policy of all Europe is adverse to the reception of our agricultural produce, so far as it comes into collision with its own; and, under that limitation, we are absolutely forbid to enter their ports, except under circumstances which deprive them of all value as a steady market. The policy of all Europe rejects those great staples of our country, which consist of objects of human subsistence. The policy of all Europe refuses to receive from us any thing but those raw materials of smaller value, essential to their manufactures, to which they can give a higher value, with the exception of tobacco and rice, which they cannot produce. Even Great Britain, to which we are its best customer, and from which we receive nearly one half in value of our whole imports, will not take from us articles of subsistence produced in our country cheaper than can be produced in Great Britain. In adopting this exclusive policy, the States of Europe do not inquire what is best for us, but what suits themselves, respectively; they do not take jurisdiction of the question of our interests, but limit the object of their legislation to that of the conservation of their own peculiar interests, leaving us free to prosecute ours as we please. They do not guide themselves by that romantic philanthropy, which we see displayed here, and which invokes us to continue to purchase the produce of foreign industry, without regard to the state or prosperity of our own, that foreigners may be pleased to purchase the few remaining articles of ours which their restrictive policy has not yet absolutely excluded from their consumption. What sort of a figure would a member of the British Parliament have made — what sort of a reception would his opposition have obtained, if he had remonstrated against the passage of the corn law, by which British consumption is limited to the breadstuffs of British production, to the entire exclusion of American, and stated that America could not, and would not, buy British manufactures, if Britain did not buy American flour? . . .

Our agricultural is our greatest interest. It ought ever to be predominant. All others should bend to it. And, in considering what is for its advantage, we should contemplate it in all its varieties, of planting, farming, and grazing. Can we do nothing to invigorate it? nothing to correct the errors of the past, and to brighten the still more unpromising prospects which lie before us? We have seen, I think, the causes of the distresses of the country. We have seen that an exclusive dependence upon the foreign market must lead to still severer distress, to impoverishment, to ruin. We must then change somewhat our course. We must give a new direction to some portion of our industry. We must speedily adopt a genuine American policy. Still cherishing a foreign market, let us create also a home market, to give further scope to the consumption of the produce of American in-

dustry. Let us counteract the policy of foreigners, and withdraw the support which we now give to their industry, and stimulate that of our own country. It should be a prominent object with wise legislators, to multiply the vocations and extend the business of society, as far as it can be done by the protection of our interests at home, against the injurious effects of foreign legislation. . . .

The creation of a home market is not only necessary to procure for our agriculture a just reward of its labors, but it is indispensable to obtain a supply of our necessary wants. If we cannot sell, we cannot buy. That portion of our population (and we have seen that it is not less than four-fifths) which makes comparatively nothing that foreigners will buy, has nothing to make purchases with from foreigners. It is in vain that we are told of the amount of our exports, supplied by the planting interest. They may enable the planting interest to supply all its wants; but they bring no ability to the interests not planting, unless, which cannot be pretended, the planting interest was an adequate vent for the surplus produce of the labor of all other interests. It is in vain to tantalize us with the greater cheapness of foreign fabrics. There must be an ability to purchase, if an article be obtained, whatever may be the price, high or low, at which it was sold. And a cheap article is as much beyond the grasp of him who has no means to buy, as a high one. Even if it were true that the American manufacturer would supply consumption at dearer rates, it is better to have his fabrics than the unattainable foreign fabrics; for it is better to be ill supplied than not supplied at all. A coarse coat, which will communicate warmth and cover nakedness, is better than no coat. The superiority of the home market results, 1st, from its steadiness and comparative certainty at all times; 2d, from the creation of reciprocal interests; 3d, from its greater security; and, lastly, from an ultimate and not distant augmentation of consumption, and, consequently, of comfort from increased quantity and reduced prices. But this home market, highly desirable as it is, can only be created and cherished by the protection of our own legislation against the inevitable prostration of our industry, which must ensue from the action of foreign policy and legislation. The effect and the value of this domestic care of our own interests will be obvious from a few facts and considerations. Let us suppose that half a million of persons are now employed abroad, in fabricating for our consumption those articles of which, by the operation of this bill, a supply is intended to be provided within ourselves. That half a million of persons are, in effect, subsisted by us; but their actual means of subsistence are drawn from foreign agriculture. If we could transport them to this country, and incorporate them in the mass of our own population, there would instantly arise a demand for an amount of provisions equal to that which would be requisite for their subsistence throughout the whole year. That demand, in the article of flour alone, would not be less than the quantity of about 900,000 barrels, besides a proportionate quantity of beef and pork, and other articles of subsistence. But 900,000 barrels of flour exceeded the entire quantity exported last year, by nearly 150,000 barrels. What activity would not this give? What cheerfulness would it not communicate to our now dispirited farming interest?

But if, instead of these five hundred thousand artisans emigrating from abroad, we give, by this bill, employment to an equal number of our own citizens now engaged in unprofitable argriculture,

or idle, from the want of business, the beneficial effect upon the productions of our farming labor would be nearly doubled. The quantity would be diminished by a subtraction of the produce from the labor of all those who should be diverted from its pursuits to manufacturing industry, and the value of the residue would be enhanced, both by that diminution and the creation of the home market to the extent supposed. And the honorable gentleman from Virginia may repress any apprehensions which he entertains, that the plough will be abandoned, and our fields remain unsown. For, under all the modifications of social industry, if you will secure to it a just reward, the greater attractions of agriculture will give to it that proud superiority which it has always maintained. If we suppose no actual abandonment of farming, but, what is most likely, a gradual and imperceptible employment of population in the business of manufacturing, instead of being compelled to resort to agriculture, the salutary effect would be nearly the same. Is any part of our common country likely to be injured by a transfer of the theatre of fabrication for our own consumption from Europe to America? All that those parts, if any there be, which will not, or cannot, engage in manufactures, should require, is, that their consumption should be well supplied; and if the objects of that consumption are produced in other parts of the Union that can manufacture, far from having, on that account, any just cause of complaint, their patriotism will and ought to inculcate a cheerful acquiescence in what essentially contributes, and is indispensably necessary, to the prosperity of the common family. . . .

Having called the attention of the Committee to the present adverse state of our country, and endeavored to point out the causes which have led to it; having shown that similar causes, wherever they exist in other countries, lead to the same adversity in their condition; and having shown that, wherever we find opposite causes prevailing, a high and animating state of national prosperity exists, the Committee will agree with me in thinking that it is the solemn duty of Government to apply a remedy to the evils which afflict our country, if it can apply one. Is there no remedy within the reach of the Government? Are we doomed to behold our industry languish and decay yet more and more? But there is a remedy, and that remedy consists in modifying our foreign policy, and in adopting a genuine American system. We must naturalize the arts in our country, and we must naturalize them by the only means which the wisdom of nations has yet discovered to be effectual — by adequate protection against the otherwise overwhelming influence of foreigners. This is only to be accomplished by the establishment of a tariff, to the consideration of which I am now brought.

And what is this tariff? It seems to have been regarded as a sort of monster, huge and deformed; a wild beast, endowed with tremendous powers of destruction, about to be let loose among our people, if not to devour them, at least to consume their substance. But let us calm our passions, and deliberately survey this alarming, this terrific being. The sole object of the tariff is to tax the produce of foreign industry, with the view of promoting American industry. The tax is exclusively levelled at foreign industry. That is the avowed and the direct purpose of the tariff. If it subjects any part of American industry to burdens, that is an effect not intended, but is altogether incidental, and perfectly voluntary.

It had been treated as an imposition of burdens upon one part of the community by design for the benefit of another; as if, in fact, money were taken from the pockets of one portion of the people and put into the pockets of another. But, is that a fair representation of it? No man pays the duty assessed on the foreign article by compulsion, but voluntarily; and this voluntary duty, if paid, goes into the common exchequer, for the common benefit of all. . . .

. . . we perceive that the proposed measure [Tariff Act of 1824], instead of sacrificing the South to the other parts of the Union, seeks only to preserve them from being absolutely sacrificed under the operation of the tacit compact which I have described. Supposing the South to be actually incompetent, or disinclined to embark at all in the business of manufacturing, is not its interest, nevertheless, likely to be promoted by creating a new and an American source of supply for its consumption? Now foreign Powers, and Great Britain principally, have the monopoly of the supply of Southern consumption. If this bill should pass, an American competitor in the supply of the South would be raised up, and ultimately, I cannot doubt, that it would be supplied cheaper and better. . . .

The second objection to the proposed bill is, that it will diminish the amount of our exports. It can have no effect upon our exports, except those which are sent to Europe. Except tobacco and rice, we send there nothing but the raw materials. The argument is, that Europe will not buy of us if we do not buy of her. The first objection to it is, that it calls upon us to look to the question, and take care of European ability in legislating for American interests. Now, if, in legislating for their interests, they would consider and provide for our ability, the principle of reciprocity would enjoin us so to regulate our intercourse with them, as to leave their ability unimpaired. But I have shown that, in the adoption of their own policy, their inquiry is strictly limited to a consideration of their peculiar interests, without any regard to that of ours. The next remark I would make is, that the bill only operates upon certain articles of European industry, which, it is supposed, our interest requires us to manufacture within ourselves; and, although its effect will be to diminish the amount of our imports of those articles, it leaves them free to supply us with any other produce of their industry. And, since the circle of human comforts, refinements, and luxuries, is of great extent, Europe will still find herself able to purchase from us what she has hitherto done, and to discharge the debt in some of those objects. If there be any diminution in our exports to Europe, it will probably be in the article of cotton to Great Britain. I have stated that Britain buys cotton wool to the amount of about five millions sterling, and sells to foreign States to the amount of upwards of twenty-one millions and a half. Of this sum, we take a little upwards of a million and a half. The residue, of about twenty millions, she must sell to other foreign Powers than the United States. Now their market will continue open to her, as much after the passage of this bill as before. She will therefore require from us the raw material to supply their consumption. But, it is said, she may refuse to purchase it of us, and seek a supply elsewhere. There can be but little doubt that she now resorts to us, because we can supply her cheaper and better than any other country. And it would be unreasonable to suppose that she would cease, from any pique towards us, to pursue her own interest. Suppose she was to decline purchasing from us: The consequence would be, that she would lose the market for the twenty millions ster-

ling which she now sells other foreign Powers, or enter into it under a disadvantageous competition with us, or with other nations, who should obtain their supplies of the raw material from us. If there should be any diminution, therefore, in the exportation of cotton, it would only be in the proportion of about one and a half to twenty, that is, a little upwards of five per cent.; the loss of a market for which, abroad, would be fully compensated by the market for the article created at home. Lastly, I would observe, that the new application of our industry, producing new objects of exportation, and they possessing much greater value than in the raw state, we should be in the end amply indemnified, by their exportation. Already the item in our foreign exports of manufactures is considerable; and we know that our cotton fabrics have been recently exported, in a large amount, to South America, where they maintain a successful competition with those of any other country.

The third objection to the tariff is, that it will diminish our navigation. This great interest deserves every encouragement consistent with the paramount interest of agriculture. In the order of nature it is secondary to both agriculture and manufactures. Its business is the transportation of the productions of those two superior branches of industry. It cannot therefore be expected that they shall be moulded or sacrificed to suit its purposes; but, on the contrary, navigation must accommodate itself to the actual state of agriculture and manufactures. If, as I believe, we have nearly reached the maximum in value of our exports of raw produce to Europe, the effect hereafter will be, as it respects that branch of our trade, if we persevere in the foreign system, to retain our navigation at the point it has now reached. By reducing, indeed, as will probably take place, the price of our raw materials, a further quantity of them could be exported, and of course additional employment might in that way be given to our tonnage; but that would be at the expense of the agricultural interest. If I am right in supposing that no effect will be produced by this measure upon any other branch of our export trade but that to Europe; that with regard to that there will be no sensible diminution of our exports, and that the new direction given to a portion of our industry will produce other objects of exportation, the probability is, that our foreign tonnage will be even increased under the operation of this bill. But, if I am mistaken in these views, and it should experience any reduction, the increase of our coasting tonnage, resulting from the greater activity of domestic exchanges, will more than compensate the injury. Although our navigation partakes in the general distress of the country, it is less depressed than any other of our great interests. The foreign tonnage has been gradually, though slowly, increasing since 1818. And our coasting tonnage since 1816 has increased upwards of one hundred thousand tons. . . .

[Fourth Objection] But, according to the opponents of the domestic policy, the proposed system will force capital and labor into new and reluctant employments; we are not prepared, in consequence of the high price of wages, for the successful establishment of manufactures, and we must fail in the experiment. We have seen that the existing occupations of our society, those of agriculture, commerce, navigation, and the learned professions, are overflowing with competitors, and that the want of employment is severely felt. Now what does this bill propose? To open a new and extensive field of business, in which all that choose

may enter. There is no compulsion upon any one to engage in it. An option only is given to industry, to continue in the present unprofitable pursuits, or to embark in a new and promising one. The effect will be to lessen the competition in the old branches of business, and to multiply our resources for increasing our comforts and augmenting the national wealth. The alleged fact of the high price of wages is not admitted. The truth is, that no class of society suffers more, in the present stagnation of business, than the laboring class. That is a necessary effect of the depression of agriculture, the principal business of the community. The wages of able-bodied men vary from five to eight dollars per month; and such has been the want of employment, in some parts of the Union, that instances have not been unfrequent, of men working merely for the means of present subsistence. If the wages for labor here and in England are compared, they will be found not to be essentially different. I agree with the honorable gentleman from Virginia, that high wages are a proof of national prosperity; we differ only in the means by which that desirable end shall be attained. But, if the fact were true, that the wages of labor are high, I deny the correctness of the argument founded upon it. The argument assumes, that natural labor is the principal element in the business of manufacture. That was the ancient theory. But the valuable inventions and vast improvements in machinery, which have been made within a few years past, have produced a new era in the arts. The effect of this change in the powers of production may be estimated from what I have already stated in relation to England, and to the triumphs of European artificial labor over the natural labor of Asia. In considering the fitness of a nation for the establishment of manufactures, we must no longer limit our views to the state of its population, and the price of wages. All circumstances must be regarded, of which that is, perhaps, the least important. Capital, ingenuity in the construction, and adroitness in the use of machinery, and the possession of the raw materials, are those which deserve the greatest consideration. All these circumstances, (except that of capital, of which there is no deficiency,) exist in our country in an eminent degree, and more than counterbalance the disadvantage, if it really existed, of the lower wages of labor in Great Britain. . . .

[Fifth Objection] But it is said, that wherever there is a concurrence of favorable circumstances, manufactures will arise of themselves, without protection; and that we should not disturb the natural progress of industry, but leave things to themselves. If all nations would modify their policy on this axiom, perhaps it would be better for the common good of the whole. Even then, in consequence of natural advantages, and a greater advance in civilization and in the arts, some nations would enjoy a state of much higher prosperity than others. But there is no universal legislation. The globe is divided into different communities, each seeking to appropriate to itself all the advantages it can, without reference to the prosperity of others. Whether this is right or not, it has always been, and ever will be, the case. Perhaps the care of the interests of our people is sufficient for all the wisdom of one Legislature; and that it is among nations as among individuals, that the happiness of the whole is best secured by each attending to its own peculiar interests. The proposition to be maintained by our adversaries, is, that manufactures, without protection, will, in due time, spring up in our country, and sustain themselves, in a competition with foreign fabrics, however advanced the arts, and whatever the degree of protection may be in foreign countries. Now I contend that this proposition is refuted by all experience, ancient and modern, and in every country. If I am asked, why unprotected industry should not succeed in a struggle with protected industry, I answer, the *fact* has ever been so, and that is sufficient; I reply that *uniform experience* evinces that it cannot succeed in such an unequal contest and that is sufficient. If we speculate on the causes of this universal truth, we may differ about them. Still the indisputable fact remains. And we should be as unwise in not availing ourselves of the guide which it furnishes, as a man would be who should refuse to bask in the rays of the sun, because he could not agree with Judge Woodward as to the nature of the substance of that planet, to which we are indebted for heat and light. If I were to attempt to particularize the causes which prevent the success of the manufacturing arts, without protection, I should say that they are — first, the obduracy of fixed habits. No nation, no individual, will easily change an established course of business, even if it be unprofitable; and least of all is an agricultural people prone to innovation. With what reluctance do they not adopt improvements in the instruments of husbandry or in modes of cultivation! If the farmer makes a good crop, and sells it badly, or makes a short crop, buoyed up by hope, he perseveres, and trusts that a favorable change of the market, or of the season, will enable him, in the succeeding year, to repair the misfortunes of the past. Secondly, the uncertainty, fluctuation, and unsteadiness, of the home market, when liable to an unrestricted influx of fabrics from all foreign nations; and, thirdly, the superior advance of skill, and amount of capital, which foreign nations have obtained, by the protection of their own industry. From the latter, or from other causes, the unprotected manufactures of a country are exposed to the danger of being crushed in their infancy, either by the design or from the necessities of foreign manufacturers. Gentlemen are incredulous as to the attempts of foreign merchants and manufacturers to accomplish the destruction of ours. Why should they not make such attempts? If the Scottish manufacturer, by surcharging our market, in one year, with the article of cotton bagging, for example, should so reduce the price as to discourage and put down the home manufacture, he would secure to himself the monopoly of the supply. And now having the exclusive possession of the market, perhaps for a long term of years, he might be more than indemnified for his first loss, in the subsequent rise in the price of the article. . . .

[Seventh Objection] But if the policy of protection be wise, the gentleman from Virginia (Mr. Barbour) has made some ingenious calculations to prove that the measure of protection, already extended, has been sufficiently great. With some few exceptions, the existing duties, of which he has made an estimate, were laid with the object of revenue, and without reference to that of encouragement to our domestic industry; and, although it is admitted that the incidental effect of duties, so laid, is to promote manufactures, yet, if it falls short of competent protection, the duties might as well not have been imposed with reference to that purpose. A moderate addition may accomplish this desirable end; and the proposed tariff is believed to have this character.

[Eighth Objection] The prohibitory policy, it is confidently asserted, is condemned by the wisdom of Europe, and by her most enlightened statesmen. Is this the fact? We call upon gentlemen to show, in what instance, a nation that has enjoyed its benefits, has surrendered it. . . .

But, is it true that England is convinced of the impolicy of the prohibitory system, and desirous to abandon it? What proof have we to that effect? We are asked to reject the evidence, deducible from the settled and steady practice of England, and to take lessons in a school of philosophical writers, whose visionary theories are no where adopted; or, if adopted, bring with them inevitable distress, impoverishment, and ruin. . . .

[Ninth Objection] The next objection of the honorable gentleman from Virginia, which I shall briefly notice, is, that the manufacturing system is adverse to the genius of our Government, in its tendency to the accumulation of large capitals in a few hands; in the corruption of the public morals, which is alleged to be incident to it; and in the consequent danger to the public liberty. The first part of the objection would apply to every lucrative business — to commerce, to planting, and to the learned professions. Would the gentleman introduce the system of Lycurgus? If his principle be correct, it should be extended to any and every vocation which had a similar tendency. The enormous fortunes in our country — the nabobs of the land — have been chiefly made by the profitable pursuit of that foreign commerce, in more propitious times, which the honorable gentleman would so carefully cherish. Immense estates have also been made in the South. The dependants are, perhaps, not more numerous upon that wealth which is accumulated in manufactures, than they are upon that which is acquired by commerce and by agriculture. We may safely confide in the laws of distributions, and in the absence of the rule of primogeniture, for the dissipation (perhaps too rapid) of large fortunes. What has become of those which were held two or three generations back in Virginia? Many of the descendants of the ancient aristocracy (as it was called) of that State, are now in the most indigent condition. The best security against the demoralization of society is the constant and profitable employment of its members. The greatest danger to public liberty is from idleness and vice. If manufactures form cities, so does commerce. And the disorders and violence which proceed from the contagion of the passions are as frequent in one description of those communities as in the other. There is no doubt but that the yeomanry of a country is the safest depository of public liberty. In all time to come, and under any probable direction of the labor of our population, the agricultural class must be much the most numerous and powerful, and will ever retain (as it ought to retain) a preponderating influence in our councils. The extent and the fertility of our lands constitute an adequate security against an excess in manufactures; and also against oppression on the part of capitalists towards the laboring portions of the community. . . .

We have had great difficulties to en-counter. 1. The splendid talents which are arrayed in this House against us. 2. We are opposed by the rich and powerful in the land. 3. The Executive Government, if any, affords us but a cold and equivocal support. 4. The importing and navigating interests, I verily believe from misconception, are adverse to us. 5. The British factors and the British influence are inimical to our success. 6. Long established habits and prejudices oppose us. 7. The reviewers and literary speculators, foreign and domestic. And, lastly, the leading presses of the country, including the influence of that which is established in this city, and sustained by the public purse.

From some of these, or other causes, the bill may be postponed, thwarted, defeated. But the cause is the cause of the country, and it must and will prevail. It is founded in the interests and affections of the people. It is as native as the granite deeply embosomed in our mountains. And, in conclusion, I would pray God, in His infinite mercy, to avert from our country the evils which are impending over it, and, by enlightening our councils, to conduct us into that path which leads to riches, to greatness, to glory.

Daniel Webster of Massachusetts

. . . I am bound to say that Mr. Speaker [Henry Clay] began this able and impressive speech at the proper point of inquiry; I mean the present state and condition of the country; although I am so unfortunate, or rather, although I am so happy, as to differ from him very widely in regard to that condition. I dissent entirely from the justice of that picture of distress which he has drawn. I have not seen the reality, and know not where it exists. Within my observation there is no cause for so gloomy and terrifying a representation. In respect to the New England States, with the condition of which I am, of course, most acquainted, the present appears to me a period of very general prosperity. Not, indeed, a time for great profits and sudden acquisition; not a day of extraordinary activity and successful

Annals of Congress, ibid., April 2, 1824, pp. 2028–2068.

speculation. There is, no doubt, a considerable depression of prices, and, in some degree, a stagnation of business. But the case presented by Mr. Speaker was not one of depression, but of distress; of universal, pervading, intense distress, limited to no class, and to no place. We are represented as on the very verge and brink of national ruin. So far from acquiescing in these opinions, I believe there has been no period in which the general prosperity was better secured, or rested on a more solid foundation. As applicable to the Eastern States, I put this remark to their Representatives, and ask them if it is not true. When has there been a time in which the means of living have been more accessible and more abundant? when labor was rewarded, I do not say with a larger, but with a more certain success? Profits, indeed, are lower; in some pursuits of life, which it is not proposed to benefit, but to burden, by this bill, very low. But still I am unacquainted with any proofs of extraordinary distress. What, indeed, are the general indications of the state of the country? There is no famine nor pestilence in the land, nor war, nor desolation. There is no writhing under the burden of taxation. The means of subsistence are abundant; and at the very moment when the miserable condition of the country is asserted, it is admitted that the wages of labor are high, in comparison with those of any other country. A country, then, enjoying a profound peace, a perfect civil liberty, with the means of subsistence cheap and abundant, with the reward of labor sure, and its wages higher than anywhere else, cannot be represented in gloom, melancholy, and distress, but by the effort of extraordinary powers of tragedy. . . .

In forming an opinion of the degree of general prosperity, we may regard, . . .

the progress of internal improvements, the investment of capital in roads, bridges, and canals. All these prove a balance of income over expenditure; they are evidence that there is a surplus of profits, which the present generation is usefully vesting for the benefit of the next. It cannot be denied that, in this particular, the progress of the country is steady and rapid.

We may look, too, to the expenses of education. Are our colleges deserted? Do fathers find themselves less able than usual to educate their children? It will be found, I imagine, that the amount paid for the purpose of education is constantly increasing, and that the schools and colleges were never more full than at the present moment. I may add that the endowment of public charities, the contributions to objects of general benevolence, whether foreign or domestic, the munificence of individuals towards what ever promises to benefit the community, are all so many proofs of national prosperity. And, finally, there is no defalcation of revenue, no pressure of taxation.

The general result, therefore, of a fair examination of the present condition of things, seems to me to be that there is a considerable depression of prices and curtailment of profit; and, in some parts of the country, it must be admitted there is a great degree of pecuniary embarrassment, arising from the difficulty of paying debts which were contracted when prices were high. With these qualifications, the general state of the country may be said to be prosperous; and these are not sufficient to give to the whole face of affairs any appearance of general distress.

Supposing the evil, then, to be a depression of prices, and a partial pecuniary pressure, the next inquiry is into the causes of that evil; and it appears to me that there are several; and, in this respect, I think, too much has been imputed, by Mr. Speaker, to the single cause of the diminution of exports. Connected, as we are, with all the commercial nations of the world, and having observed great changes to take place elsewhere, we should consider whether the causes of those changes have not reached us, and whether we are not suffering by the operation of those causes, in common with others. Undoubtedly there has been a great fall in the price of all commodities throughout the commercial world, in consequence of the restoration of a state of peace. When the allies entered France in 1814, prices rose astonishingly fast and very high. Colonial produce, for instance, in the ports of this country, as well as elsewhere, sprung up suddenly from the lowest to the highest extreme. A new and vast demand was created for the commodities of trade. These were the natural consequences of the great political changes which then took place in Europe.

We are to consider, too, that our own war created new demand, and that a Government expenditure of 25,000,000 or 30,000,000 a year, had the usual effect of enhancing prices. We are obliged to add, that the paper issues of our banks carried the same effect still further. . . .

. . . The year 1819 was a year of numerous failures, and very considerable distress, and would have furnished far better grounds than exist at present, for that gloomy representation of our condition which has been presented. Mr. Speaker has alluded to the strong inclination which exists, or has existed, in various parts of the country to issue paper money, as a proof of great existing difficulties. I regard it rather as a very productive cause of those difficulties; and the Committee will not fail to observe, that there is, at this moment, much the loudest complaint of distress precisely where there has been the greatest attempt to relieve it by systems of paper credit. And, on the other hand, content, prosperity, and happiness, are most observable in those parts of the country, where there has been the least endeavor to administer relief by law. . . . I regard, sir, this issue of irredeemable paper as the most prominent and deplorable cause of whatever pressure still exists in the country; and, further, I would put the question to the members of this Committee, whether it is not from that part of the people who have tried this paper system, and tried it to their cost, that this bill receives the most earnest support? And I cannot forbear to ask, further, whether this support does not proceed rather from a general feeling of uneasiness under the present condition of things, than from the clear perception of any benefit which the measure itself can confer? . . . The depression of prices and the stagnation of business, have been in truth the necessary result of circumstances. No Government could prevent them, and no Government can altogether relieve the people from their effect. We had enjoyed a day of extraordinary prosperity; we had been neutral while the world was at war, and had found a great demand for our products, our navigation, and our labor. We had no right to expect that that state of things would continue always. With the return to peace, foreign nations would struggle for themselves, and enter into competition with us in the great objects of pursuit.

Now, sir, what is the remedy for existing evils? what is the course of policy suited to our actual condition? Certainly it is not our wisdom to adopt any system that may be offered to us without examination, and in the blind hope that whatever *changes* our condition may improve it. It is better that we should

"Bear those ills we have,
Than fly to others that we know not of."

We are bound to see that there is a fitness and an aptitude in whatever measures may be recommended to relieve the evils that afflict us; and before we adopt a system that professes to make great alterations, it is our duty to look carefully to each leading interest of the community, and see how it may probably be affected by our proposed legislation.

And, in the first place, what is the condition of our commerce? Here we must clearly perceive that it is not enjoying that rich harvest which fell to its fortune during the continuance of the European wars. It has been greatly depressed, and limited to small profits. Still, it is elastic and active, and seems capable of recovering itself in some measure from its depression. The shipping interest, also, has suffered severely, still more severely, probably, than commerce. If any thing should strike us with astonishment, it is that the navigation of the United States should be able to sustain itself. Without any Government protection whatever, it goes abroad to challenge competition with the whole world; and, in spite of all obstacles, it has yet been able to maintain 800,000 tons in the employment of foreign trade. How, sir, do the ship-owners and navigators accomplish this? How is it that they are able to meet, and in some measure overcome, universal competition? Not, sir, by protection and bounties; but by unwearied exertion, by extreme economy, by unshaken perseverance, by that manly and resolute spirit which relies on itself to protect itself. These causes alone enable American ships still to keep their element, and show the flag of their country in distant seas. The

rates of insurance may teach us how thoroughly our ships are built, and how skilfully and safely they are navigated. Risks are taken, as I learn, from the United States to Liverpool, at one per cent.; and from the United States to Canton and back, as low as three per cent. But when we look to the low rate of freight, and when we consider, also, that the articles entering into the composition of a ship, with the exception of wood, are dearer here than in other countries, we cannot but be utterly surprised that the shipping interest has been able to sustain itself at all. I need not say that the navigation of the country is essential to its honor and its defence. Yet, instead of proposing benefit for it in this hour of its depression, we propose by this measure to lay upon it new and heavy burdens. In the discussion, the other day, of that provision of the bill which proposes to tax tallow for the benefit of the oil merchants and whalemen, we had the pleasure of hearing eloquent eulogiums upon that portion of our shipping employed in the whale fishery, and strong statements of its importance to the public interest. But the same bill proposes a severe tax upon that interest for the benefit of the iron manufacturer and the hemp grower. So that the tallow chandlers and soap boilers are sacrificed to the oil merchants, in order that these again may contribute to the manufacturers of iron and the growers of hemp.

If such be the state of our commerce and navigation, what is the condition of our home manufactures? How are they amidst the general depression? Do they need further protection? and if any, how much? On all these points, we have had much general statement, but little precise information. In the very elaborate speech of Mr. Speaker, we are not supplied with satisfactory grounds of judging in these various particulars. Who can tell, from any thing yet before the Committee, whether the proposed duty be too high or too low on any one article? Gentlemen tell us that they are in favor of domestic industry; so am I. They would give it protection; so would I. But then all domestic industry is not confined to manufactures. The employments of agriculture, commerce, and navigation, are all branches of the same domestic industry; they all furnish employment for American capital and American labor. And when the question is, whether new duties shall be laid, for the purpose of giving further encouragement to particular manufactures, every reasonable man must ask himself, both, whether the proposed new encouragement be necessary, and, whether it can be given without injustice to other branches of industry. . . .

I will now proceed, sir, to state some objections which I feel, of a more general nature, to the course of Mr. Speaker's observations.

He seems to me to argue the question as if all domestic industry were confined to the production of manufactured articles; as if the employment of our own capital, and our own labor, in the occupations of commerce and navigation, were not as emphatically domestic industry as any other occupation. Some other gentlemen, in the course of the debate, have spoken of the price paid for every foreign manufactured article, as so much given for the encouragement of foreign labor, to the prejudice of our own. But is not every such article the product of our own labor as truly as if we had manufactured it ourselves? Our labor has earned it, and paid the price for it. It is so much added to the stock of national wealth. If the commodity were dollars, nobody would doubt the truth of this remark: and it is precisely as correct in its application to any other

commodity as to silver. One man makes a yard of cloth at home; another raises agricultural products, and buys a yard of imported cloth. Both these are equally the earnings of domestic industry, and the only questions that arise in the case are two: the first is, which is the best mode, under all the circumstances, of obtaining the article; the second is, how far this first question is proper to be decided by Government, and how far it is proper to be left to individual discretion. There is no foundation for the distinction which attributes to certain employments the peculiar appellation of American industry; and it is, in my judgment, extremely unwise, to attempt such discriminations. We are asked, what nations have ever attained eminent prosperity without encouraging manufactures? I may ask, what nation ever reached the like prosperity without promoting foreign trade? I regard these interests as closely connected, and am of opinion that it should be our aim to cause them to flourish together. I know it would be very easy to promote manufactures, at least for a time, but probably only for a short time, if we might act in disregard of other interests. We could cause a sudden transfer of capital, and a violent change in the pursuits of men. We could exceedingly benefit some classes by these means. But what, then, becomes of the interests of others? The power of collecting revenue by duties on imports, and the habit of the Government of collecting almost its whole revenue in that mode, will enable us, without exceeding the bounds of moderation, to give great advantages to those classes of manufactures which we may think most useful to promote at home. What I object to is the immoderate use of the power — exclusions and prohibitions; all of which, as I think, not only interrupt the pursuits of individuals, with great injury to themselves, and little or no benefit to the country, but also often divert our own labor, or, as it may very properly be called, our own domestic industry, from those occupations in which it is well employed and well paid, to others, in which it will be worse employed, and worse paid. . . .

Let me now ask, sir, what relief this bill proposes to some of those great and essential interests of the country, the condition of which has been referred to as proof of national distress; and which condition, although I do not think it makes out a case of distress, yet does indicate depression.

And first, as to our foreign trade. The Speaker has stated that there has been a considerable falling off in the tonnage employed in that trade. This is true, lamentably true. In my opinion, it is one of those occurrences which ought to arrest our immediate, our deep, our most earnest attention. What does this bill propose for its relief? Sir, it proposes nothing but new burdens. It proposes to diminish its employment, and it proposes, at the same time, to augment its expense, by subjecting it to heavier taxation. Sir, there is no interest, in regard to which a stronger case for protection can be made out, than the navigating interest. Whether we look at its present condition, which is admitted to be depressed; the number of persons connected with it, and dependent upon it for their daily bread; or its importance to the country in a political point of view, it has claims upon our attention which cannot be exceeded. But what do we propose to do for it? I repeat, sir, simply to burden and to tax it. By a statement which I have already submitted to the Committee, it appears that the shipping interest pays, annually, more than half a million of dollars in duties on articles used in the construction of ships. We propose to add nearly, or quite, fifty per cent. to this amount, at the very moment that we

bring forth the languishing state of this interest, as a proof of national distress. Let it be remembered that our shipping employed in foreign commerce, has, at this moment, not the shadow of Government protection. It goes abroad upon the wide sea to make its own way, and earn its own bread, in a professed competition with the whole world. Its resources are its own frugality, its own skill, its own enterprise. It hopes to succeed, if it shall succeed at all, not by extaordinary aid of Government, but by patience, vigilance, and toil. This right arm of the nation's safety strengthens its own muscle by its own efforts, and by unwearied exertion in its own defence becomes strong for the defence of the country. . . .

Again, Mr. Chairman, the failures and the bankruptcies which have taken place in our large cities have been mentioned as proving the little success attending commerce and its general decline. But this bill has no balm for those wounds. It is very remarkable, that, when losses and disasters of certain manufacturers, those of iron, for instance, are mentioned, it is done for the purpose of invoking aid for the distressed. Not so with the losses and disasters of commerce; these last are narrated, and not unfrequently much exaggerated, to prove the ruinous nature of the employment, and to show that it ought to be abandoned, and the capital engaged in it turned to other objects. . . .

The true course then, sir, for us to pursue, is, in my opinion, to consider what our situation is, what our means are, and how they can be best applied. What amount of population have we, in comparison with our extent of soil, what amount of capital and labor, at what price? As to skill, knowledge, and enterprise, we may safely take it for granted, that, in these particulars, we are on an equality with others. Keeping these considerations in view, allow me to examine two or three of those provisions of the bill to which I feel the strongest objections.

To begin with the article of iron. Our whole annual consumption of this article is supposed by the chairman of the committee to be 48,000 or 50,000 tons. Let us suppose the latter. The amount of our own manufacture he estimates, I think, at 17,000 tons. The present duty on the imported article is $15 per ton, and as this duty causes, of course, an equivalent augmentation of the price of the home manufacture, the whole increase of price is equal to $750,000 annually. This sum we pay on a raw material, and on an absolute necessary of life. The bill proposes to raise the duty from $15 to $22½ per ton, which would be equal to $1,125,000 on the whole annual consumption. So that, suppose the point of prohibition which is aimed at by some gentlemen to be attained, the consumers of the article would pay this last mentioned sum every year to the producers of it, over and above the price at which they could supply themselves with the same article from other sources. There would be no mitigation of this burden, except from the prospect, whatever that might be, that iron would fall in value, by domestic competition, after the importation should be prohibited. It will be easy, I think, to show that it cannot fall; and supposing for the present that it shall not, the result will be, that we shall pay annually a sum of $1,125,000, constantly augmented, too, by increased consumption of the article, *to support a business that cannot support itself*. It is of no consequence to the argument that this sum is expended at home; so it would be, if we taxed the people to support any other useless and expensive establishment, to build another Capitol for example, or incur an unnecessary expense of any sort. The question still is, are the money, time, and labor, well laid out in these cases? The present price of iron at Stockholm, I am assured by importers, is $53 per ton on board, $48 per ton in the yard before loading, and probably not far from $40 at the mines. Freight, insurance, &c., may be fairly estimated at $15, to which add our present duty of $15 more, and these two last sums, together with the cost on board at Stockholm, give $83 as the cost of Swedes iron in our market. In fact it is said to have been sold last year at $81½ to $82 per ton. We perceive, by this statement, that the cost of iron is doubled in reaching us from the mine in which it is produced. In other words, our present duty, with the expense of transportation, gives an advantage to the American over the foreign manufacturer, of one hundred per cent. Why, then, cannot the iron be manufactured at home? Our ore is said to be as good, and some of it better. It is under our feet, and the chairman of the committee tells us that it might be wrought by persons who otherwise will not be employed. *Why, then, is it not wrought?* Nothing could be more sure of constant sale. It is not an article of changeable fashion, but of absolute, permanent necessity, and such, therefore, as would always meet a steady demand. Sir, I think it would be well for the chairman of the committee to revise his premises, for I am persuaded that there is an ingredient properly belonging to the calculation which he has misstated or omitted. Swedes iron in England pays a duty, I think, of about $27 per ton; yet it is imported in considerable quantities, notwithstanding the vast capital, the excellent coal, and, more important than all, perhaps, the highly improved state of inland navigation in England; although I am aware that the English use of Swedes iron may be thought to be owing in some degree to its superior quality.

Sir, the true explanation of this appears to me to lie in the different prices *of labor;* and here, I apprehend, is the grand mistake in the argument of the chairman of the committee. He says it would cost the nation, as a nation, nothing to make our ore into iron. Now, I think, it would cost us precisely that which we can worst afford; that is, *great labor.* Although bar iron is very properly considered a raw material in respect to its various future uses, yet, as bar iron, the principal ingredient in its cost is labor. Of manual labor, no nation has more than a certain quantity, nor can it be increased at will. As to some operations, indeed, its place may be supplied by machinery; but there are other services which machinery cannot perform for it, and which it must perform for itself. A most important question for every nation, as well as for every individual to propose to itself, is, how it can best apply that quantity of labor which it is able to perform?

Labor is the great producer of wealth; it moves all other causes. If it call machinery to its aid, it is still employed, not only in using the machinery, but in making it. Now, with respect to the quantity of labor, as we all know, different nations are differently circumstanced. Some need, more than any thing, work for hands; others require hands for work; and, if we ourselves are not absolutely in the latter class, we are still, most fortunately, very near it. I cannot find that we have those idle hands, of which the chairman of the committee speaks. The price of labor is a conclusive and unanswerable refutation of that idea; it is known to be higher with us than in any other civilized State, and this is the greatest of all proofs of general happiness. Labor in this country is independent and proud. It has not to ask the patronage of capital, but capital solicits the aid of labor. This is the general truth,

in regard to the condition of our whole population, although in the large cities there are, doubtless, many exceptions. The mere capacity to labor in common agricultural employments gives to our young men the assurance of independence. We have been asked, sir, by the chairman of the committee, in a tone of some pathos, whether we will allow to serfs of Russia and Sweden the benefit of making iron for us? Let me inform the gentleman, sir, that those same serfs do not earn more than *seven cents* a day, and that they work in those mines, for that compensation, because they are serfs. And, let me ask the gentleman further, whether we have any labor in this country that cannot be better employed than in a business which does not yield the laborer more than seven cents a day? This, it appears to me, is the true question for our consideration. There is no reason for saying that we will work iron because we have mountains that contain the ore. We might, for the same reason, dig among our rocks for the scattered grains of gold and silver which might be found there. The true inquiry is, can we produce the article in a useful state at the same cost, or nearly at the same cost, or at any reasonable approximation towards the same cost, at which we can import it?

Some general estimates of the price and profits of labor, in those countries from which we import our iron, might be formed by comparing the reputed products of different mines, and their prices, with the number of hands employed. The mines of Danemora are said to yield about four thousand tons, and to employ in the mines twelve hundred workmen. Suppose this to be worth fifty dollars per ton; any one will find, by computation, that the whole product would not pay, in this country, for one-quarter part of the necessary labor. The whole export of Sweden was estimated, a few years ago, at 400,000 ship-pounds, or about 54,000 tons. Comparing this product with the number of workmen usually supposed to be employed in the mines which produce iron for exportation, the result will not greatly differ from the foregoing. These estimates are general, and might not conduct us to a precise result; but we know, from intelligent travellers, and eye-witnesses, that the price of labor, in the Swedish mines, does not exceed seven cents a day.

The true reason, sir, why it is not our policy to compel our citizens to manufacture our own iron, is, that they are far better employed. It is an unproductive business, and they are not poor enough to be obliged to follow it. If we had more of poverty, more of misery, and something of servitude; if we had an ignorant, idle, starving, population, we might set up for iron makers against the world. . . .

Sir, I will detain you no longer. There are some parts of this bill which I highly approve; there are others in which I should acquiesce; but those to which I have now stated my objections appear to me so destitute of all justice, so burdensome, and so dangerous to that interest which has steadily enriched, gallantly defended, and proudly distinguished us, that nothing can prevail upon me to give it my support.

James Hamilton of South Carolina

Mr. H. said there was one consideration to be borne in mind, which was inseparably connected with the measure under discussion, and that was, the utter impossibility of satisfying the monopolists engaged in manufactures, who were so clamorous for the passage of this bill, with any thing short of absolute prohibition. They had been, by steadily marching up to this point, gathering numbers, by cunning addresses to popular prejudice and feeling, from 1790, through the several revisions of the tariff, up to the present time. It was as easy to cater for a cormorant as to satisfy their greedy appetite for gain. Their industry, combination, perseverance, and identity of interest, rendered the whole corps more dangerous to the peace and prosperity of a community than even a full and well-organized detachment of smugglers. Their avarice invariably approaches under the guise of public spirit, whilst the unity of purpose with which they act, gives an overwhelming energy to their exertions. Committees of correspondence, public meetings, and the press, more prolific than the herrings of Norway, are all united, in a "holy alliance," to fasten on the country a system which, in taxing nine-tenths of the people, is to reward their pious and patriotic efforts. . . .

. . . He would, therefore, speak of the bill and the manner in which it had been got up just as he believed they deserved. The first thing he should say, was, that he believed there had been more outdoor than indoor legislation, in regard to the measure. He feared that the sheet, now so fearfully filled up, had been, for some time before the commencement of the session, held up as a sort of *carte blanche* in which every monopolist might insert just such a tax as he wished levied on the community to encourage his pious labors. If he had understood correctly, all sorts of pilgrims had travelled to the room of the Committee on Manufactures, from the sturdy iron master down to the poor manufacturer of whetstones, all equally clamorous for the protection "of a *parental*, of an *American* policy." A friend, in whose veracity and accuracy he had great confidence, had informed him that he had seen, in a paper of one of the cities north of this, a letter from an umbrella maker, in which he boasted of his having successfully used his influence with the committee, to insert an increase of duty on umbrellas, in some way to encourage their manufacture.

Mr. H. said he would not stop to inquire whether one of these trips to the Seat of Government was as holy as a pilgrimage to Jerusalem or Mecca; but he nevertheless thought that a man might be more worthily employed at home than in journeys having for their object the transfer of other people's money into their own pockets, although the purpose might be most marvellously connected with great considerations of public utility, and the most lofty and spotless patriotism. Even if he was disposed to subscribe to the policy of the bill, he confessed he had serious distrust of its details. He believed that some one who had had the patience to count them, had ascertained that they consisted of nearly 300 items, on which an increase of duty has been laid. . . .

Now, it was a fact, he believed, of universal notoriety, that the Committee on Manufactures had not officially consulted the Secretary of the Treasury; and a bill, either most oppressively to increase or injuriously to diminish our revenue, is about to be passed, without his public sanction. This deficiency had not been supplied by the abundant knowledge of the gentleman from Pennsylvania, the chairman of the committee, (Mr. Tod,) who had been convicted, on more occa-

sions than one, of a gross ignorance of the operation, bearing, and character, of this measure. If it was indeed destined to become a law, it would be some consolation for those who are to suffer from its effects, to believe that they are not the victims of a blundering blindness. The poor wretch who suffers amputation should at least be comforted, under the knife, with a belief that his doctor knows what he is at. . . .

But, on the ground of expediency, is it nothing to weaken the attachment of one section of this confederacy to the bond of Union? Is it nothing to shake the confidence of a portion of our people in the integrity and justice of their Government? Is it nothing to sow the seeds of incurable alienation, by producing a belief that, in your policy you rather consult power than right? Ours is a Government of opinion; it is sustained by the affections of its people. The natural ties and charities of human life cannot remain unbroken under a sense of unmerited wrong. The affections of a child to a parent are sometimes snapt asunder by continued acts of injustice and unkindness. Feeble, in comparison with these, is that artificial contrivance, called a Government. Lord North contended, with a plausibility equal at least to the ingenuity which the honorable Speaker has displayed in proving the power in question, that the colonies had a virtual representation. We, nevertheless, are acquainted with the result. Let no man, however, tax me with holding incendiary doctrines. I know that South Carolina will cling to this Union as long as a plank of it floats on the troubled ocean of events. I know her lofty nationality and generous patriotism; but the honorable Speaker, when he makes his appeal to the gentlemen of the South, and calls upon us complacently to witness odious, partial, and undisguised burdens imposed upon our constituents, without even the justification of that expediency which sometimes gives a colorable pretext to injustice, asks from us an unreasonable boon. . . .

John Tod of Pennsylvania, Chairman of the Committee on Manufactures

. . . The matter and substance of the remarks upon our application for relief, have not been much helped by the manner, as far as respects the observation of one gentleman — I mean the gentleman from South Carolina, (Mr. Hamilton.) Some of those observations I did not hear. The gentleman from South Carolina, no doubt, believed me to be present. I ought to have been present. The truth is, when the gentleman from South Carolina came to a part of his speech in which he seemed to be commencing a dissertation upon the useful and sublime discoveries of the political economists, calling them, or some of them, immortal, &c., thinking I had heard all these matters before, I concluded nothing would be lost by my going to the committee-room upon some committee business, and stayed, perhaps, longer than I intended. The gentleman from South Carolina charged the Committee of Manufactures, very directly, with gross ignorance of their business; that the chairman of that committee had been repeatedly convicted of gross ignorance. I mention this matter because it is connected with something more material, and not for the sake of any personal complaint. Besides, the gentleman from South Carolina has already explained that part of his observations. It is proper to take this occasion to say, that the Committee of Manufactures have not yet made pretensions to any superior learning. As to myself, I know, perhaps, better than the gentleman from South Carolina, my own inadequacy to this station. It is a station which was not sought for, nor wished for, by me. It certainly found me very unprepared. Much was to be learned; and, no doubt, much yet remains unlearned. But my humility goes no further. It is not admitted that the great cause of domestic industry has suffered from any insufficiency of the Committee of Manufactures. . . .

As to the persons who have attended the Committee of Manufactures, on the invitation of the committee, or without invitation, it is due to them and to us to say, that they have all been citizens of our country, and gentlemen of good appearance and good credit. And it may be further said, that among the few of them who had any particular interest and manufacture of their own to promote, there has been scarcely one who has not gone away disappointed. . . .

Annals of Congress, ibid., April 7, 1824, pp. 2216–2218.

Andrew Stewart of Pennsylvania

. . . But commerce was represented as being on the decline, as well as agriculture and manufactures. This was, he considered, a matter of course. Commerce was the offspring of agriculture and manufactures. Where there was neither agriculture nor manufactures, there could be no commerce: they must rise and fall together. The only legitimate business of commerce was to distribute and exchange the surplus productions of labor. If by a wise policy you restore your agriculture and manufactures to their former prosperity, commerce will revive; and soon again will it be seen to spread its white bosom to the prosperous breeze. But, even if this measure should have the effect of lessening the foreign carrying trade, still we would be more than compensated by the increase of internal commerce and the coasting trade. But, would it be seriously contended that we should import what we do not want, for the sake of employing foreign commerce? Was it consistent with sound policy to import our iron from Russia, when we could produce it at home, merely to employ commerce? As well might it be contended that we ought to export our flour to England, and have it manufactured into bread, and reimported, to keep navigation and commerce employed! And this would not be more absurd and ruinous than much of the system now in operation.

Mr. S. begged leave here to notice anther argument which had been urged, not only against the duty now under consideration, but against the bill generally. It was this: that the proposed measure would operate injuriously on the farmers — that it was "taxing the many for the benefit of the few." The effect, Mr. S. contended, would be directly the reverse — it would benefit the farmers much more than the manufacturers. To simplify his views on this point, he said, he would confine them to a single county, in which he would suppose there to be at present a single manufacturing establishment, employing 100 hands, consuming $10,000 worth of grain and other agricultural productions, and making $20,000 worth of the manufactured article; and then suppose, that, by the operation of this measure, there should spring up in this county ten new and rival establishments, of equal extent, — you thus withdraw 1,000 hands from agricultural employment, and make them consumers instead of producers. You give the farmers an increased market, to the amount of $100,000; and you save $200,000 a year in one county, which is kept in profitable circulation at home, giving life and activity to every branch of industry, instead of being sent to support the industry of England, who, by her existing laws, will not suffer her people to consume a pound of our flour, even if it were offered at fifty cents a barrel? This, Mr. S. contended, was the plain and obvious tendency of the great measure under discussion. And which, he begged leave to ask, was the most benefited, the farmer or the manufacturer? Undoubtedly the farmer. The increased market, and increased demand for his produce, necessarily increased the price; while the increased competition among the manufacturers, and the increased quantity of the manufactured article thrown into the market, as inevitably diminished the price; — so that the farmer would get more for his grain, and give less for his manufactured goods. Yet,

Annals of Congress, ibid., April 9, 1824, pp. 2278–2287.

with these plain results before us, it was still gravely urged upon the House by almost every honorable gentleman who had opposed this bill. It was a principal ground of opposition, that it would "ruin the farmers — tax the many for the benefit of the few — create monopolies — enable the rich manufacturer to extort from the people," &c. — while, in fact, its real tendency and effect was, he contended, precisely the reverse.

But, Mr. S. said, there was another and still stronger view of this subject, in relation to its effects upon the interest of the farmer and agriculturist. It was a fact, however strange it might appear, susceptible of the clearest demonstration, that this nation, almost entirely agricultural, instead of exporting, actually imported agricultural labor from the poor and wretched countries of Europe to the amount of twenty or thirty millions a year. He did not mean to say that it was imported in its rude and original shape, but it entered into the composition of manufactures, and, thus altered and modified, was imported and consumed among us. Sir, of what is your imported cloth composed? your imported iron, spirits, hemp, linen — in short, almost every thing? Count the cost of the raw material, the wool, hemp, flax; then add the price of the provisions, the bread, meat, fuel, &c., consumed by those employed in the fabrication of the manufactured articles, and you will find that one-half, nay, two-thirds of the price of our imported goods consisted of agricultural labor, and went to support and sustain the farmers of foreign countries, of England, France, and Russia; while our own, shut out from Europe, and shamefully abandoned at home, were left without a market, and without a motive to industry. With an almost unlimited extent of fertile territory, abounding with the finest soil and most delightful pastures, we were importing even *grass* from foreign countries in the shape of tallow and wool. Last year we had imported vast quantities of both; four million pounds of tallow, equal to the product of 80,000 cattle. And, was it wise in this nation, where eighty-three per cent. of the whole population were employed in agriculture, to import twenty or thirty millions of dollars' worth of agricultural produce every year, in the shape of manufactures from abroad, and most of it from England, whose territory was not much larger than some of our States, and where the proportion of agriculturists was not equal to one-third of her population? The immense sums, thus sent to Europe, he argued, were *worse* than thrown away, for the amount was not only *lost* to the country, but it introduced the labor and industry of other countries to paralyze and destroy our own. He compared it to the money expended by an individual in the purchase of spirituous liquor, or other deleterious drugs, the use of which impaired the health and ruined the constitution; in both cases, the loss of money was the smallest part of the evil. These being the effects of the present system on the farmers, any change would be to them desirable — it might be for the better, it could not be for the worse.

The honorable gentleman from Massachusetts (Mr. Webster) has been pleased to denounce the restrictive policy as unwise and injudicious. He, Mr. S., would respectfully ask the honorable gentleman to point to the country which, neglecting the protection and encouragement of its own industry, and depending on foreign labor and skill for the supply of its wants, was not ultimately ruined? . . . The opposition to this measure, Mr. S. said, sprung from two sources: The commercial interest on the seaboard, and the cotton and tobacco planting interest in the South;

the first from an unfounded, though sincere apprehension, that it would diminish the business and increase the burdens of commerce and navigation; the second from an apprehension, no doubt equally sincere, but equally unfounded, that, if we cease to purchase from Europe what we can and ought to make for ourselves, Europe will cease to purchase their cotton and tobacco, which now constituted three-fourths of the whole agricultural exports of this Union. These two powerful interests had hitherto governed this nation, and dictated its policy. The interior, and the West, until lately, constituting but a small part of the great concern, of course had to submit; but, having now arrived at the age of discretion, they claimed a right to participate in the administration of the Government. They were opposed to the present ruinous system of policy, which was predicated on a state of war in Europe. While all Europe was in arms — when Kings, abandoning all other pursuits, were contending in fields of blood for kingdoms, crowns, and diadems, the United States, enjoying an unbounded market, grew rich at their expense. But Europe had changed in her condition; instead of universal war, there is now universal peace; millions of men had exchanged the sword for the plough; had quit war and went to work; instead of consumers they had become producers; instead of customers had become rivals; and our produce was not only excluded from Europe, but the rival commodities had, in many instances, followed us to our own shores. During the last year even wheat, potatoes, oats, &c., had been imported in considerable quantities; and it had become necessary to protect ourselves, by duties, against these importations; and even this (the proposed duty of twenty-five cents on wheat) had been opposed by the honorable gentleman from Massachusetts, (Mr. Webster) on the ground that the importation of foreign wheat gave additional employment to our mills, and increased the business on our canals. Our own iron works were also to be abandoned, to import our iron from Russia, for the sake of employing our "commerce and navigation!" This, he said, appeared to him to be about as wise as it would be in a Pennsylvania farmer, who, having a mill on his own farm, yet carried his grain a hundred miles into Virginia to have it ground, for the sake of employing his wagon and horses! Would it not be better for the farmer to sell his wagon, or employ it in some other way? And so he would say to the merchant.

But, sir, look at the effects of this policy — this system of free trade — "buying where we can buy cheapest." Look to what it has brought this once happy and prosperous land. With a Government the cheapest, the freest, and the best upon earth; with a country possessing every advantage of climate, situation, and soil; yet filled with monuments of misery and wretchedness, of general embarrassment, and bankruptcy, and ruin. Peace brought no relief to the farmer — none to the manufacturer; to them it brought no blessings; to the country at large it presented a cheerless prospect — of agriculture depressed, manufactures ruined, and the energies of the nation relaxed, broken, and prostrate. And even commerce, we are told by the honorable gentleman from Massachusetts, (Mr. Webster, though he contends that the country was never in a more prosperous condition,) is "scarcely able to keep its head above water." Sir, all the great interests of the country are at the lowest point of depression; they are struggling for life — sinking with agriculture, the basis and foundation of all, into a common grave. And why was this land of freedom, this home of liberty, thus clouded and o'ercast with this dark gloom and despondence, without a ray of hope to lighten or to cheer the long vista of futurity? There was no war, no famine, no plague, no taxes in the land. Could the cause then be doubtful? Did it not evidently result from our present ruinous system of policy? Was it not because the national industry was unprotected? — because we looked to Europe, instead of our own people, our own resources, for the supply of our wants? — because we buy from abroad almost every thing we eat, and drink, and wear? . . .

The strong ground, however, on which this measure was met and opposed was, that it would operate injuriously on the interests of the sugar, cotton, and tobacco planters of the South; that it would increase the price of the coarse fabrics with which they clothe their slaves, &c. This argument takes for granted the fact in controversy; a fact which he could not admit, viz., that this measure would enhance the price of the article manufactured. This he denied; and insisted that New England could, and would, manufacture the raw materials of our own country cheaper than it could be done in Europe, after being transported 3,000 miles, and encountering all the expenses of shipping and reshipping, excises, imposts, &c., to which it was subjected. When it was proposed to increase the duty upon coarse cottons, this same objection, that it was "taxing the many for the benefit of the few," was echoed in newspapers, speeches, and memorials, from Maine to Georgia. The duty was nevertheless imposed; and what has been the result? Coarse cottons, of superior quality, are now manufactured in this country, for one-half the price formerly paid to Great Britain; and now, instead of importing, we exported, last year, to the amount of $545,000 worth to foreign countries, after supplying the home consumption, amounting to many millions; which was saved and distributed among our own farmers and cotton growers, instead of going to Europe to reward foreign industry instead of our own. The same result had attended every thing that had received adequate protection — leather, nails, wood, umbrellas, shoes, boots, hats, &c.; and, from estimates made, it appeared that we saved by the manufacture of shoes, boots, and hats, alone, upwards of $34,000,000 per annum. He therefore felt warranted, by uniform experience, in the opinion, that the articles proposed to be protected by this bill — cotton, iron, coarse woollens, hemp, &c., would ultimately, and at no distant period, be furnished cheaper of American than foreign manufacture. If there was any certainty in the laws of cause and effect, this result was inevitable. But the establishment of manufactories of cotton, &c., would not only afford a market for grain and other provisions, but also for the cotton of the South; for the time might come, and was perhaps not distant, when the planter of the South might share the fate of the farmers of the Western and Middle States. They, too, might be deprived of their European market, which might be interrupted and cut off, not only by war, and the many other vicissitudes that interrupt the intercourse between nations, but it was a fact of serious import to the South, that the culture of cotton was rapidly extending itself, not only in the British islands, but also in Egypt and South America. Since 1818, the price had fallen, as appeared by the English prices current, from 28 to 7 cents a pound; our flour had also, owing to the glut of the market, fallen from $8 and $10 a barrel, to $4.50; and tobacco from $185 to $75 per hogshead.

These were some of the effects of a general peace in Europe, and they furnished powerful arguments in favor of the abandonment of a policy subject to such ruinous vicissitudes; and pointing out the necessity of adopting a permanent system of American policy, which should extend protection and encouragement to American industry, and look to American means for the supply of American wants; and if there was any nation under the sun capable of supplying all its own wants, he contended it was this. . . .

And, in conclusion, he would beg leave to appeal to the liberality, the magnanimity, to the patriotism of the enlightened Representatives of the South, who, under an ample protection, were basking in the sunshine of prosperity; and he would ask them, in a spirit of frankness and conciliation, whether they could reconcile it to their consciences to withhold the trifling protection offered in this bill to the suffering farmers and manufacturers of the interior and the West? He would appeal to the distinguished Representatives of the sugar planters of Louisiana, who, with a protecting duty of three cents a pound on sugar, were rapidly acquiring unbounded wealth and princely fortunes. He would also appeal, with the same friendly feelings, to the liberality, nay, he would say to the justice of the gentlemen from the North, who so ably represented, upon this floor, the interests of "commerce and navigation," the favored few, and he would ask them whether, while they were protected and defended, not merely by enormous discriminating duties, but also at the expense of millions of the public treasure — at the expense of the best and richest blood of this country — they would turn a deaf ear to the calls of the farmers and manufacturers, the great mass of the community, for protection, not by the sword or the purse of the nation, but by a simple act of legislation — by the passage of this bill. Sir, said Mr. S., I hope and trust the protection they ask will be granted, and granted by the votes of some of the gentlemen, at least, to whose liberality, to whose justice, to whose patriotism, he had appealed. He hoped the present destructive system of policy would now be abandoned; and, upon its ruins, there would arise a system of American policy, protecting and cherishing American industry; a policy which, in his conscience, he believed would alone save this nation from ultimate bankruptcy, and raise it to that proud pre-eminence among the nations of the earth, to which the distinguished advantages derived not only from the valor of our forefathers, but from nature, and from nature's God, give us a just right to aspire.

Samuel A. Foot of Connecticut

. . . Any attempt to force the people of these States into this silkworm policy, by the magic power of your tariff bills, will prove abortive. Their habits are too deeply rooted. The great variety and fertility of soil, the immense extent of territory, and the ocean which washes nearly three thousand miles of your coast; the majestic navigable rivers which, like the grand arteries in the human body, flow from the heart of your country to the ocean, speak a language which cannot be misunderstood, and never will be disobeyed; you must, and will, be a great

Annals of Congress, ibid., April 12, 1824, pp. 2297–2307.

agricultural and commercial nation, in spite of all your legislation.

You may, by your restrictions, embarrass and fetter their enterprise for a short period; you may legislate them into adversity, but it is impossible to legislate a people into prosperity.

The greatest degree of national and individual wealth is obtained by permitting labor, skill, and capital, to find their own employment and investment unshackled, and encourage a free and unrestricted trade. Every attempt of Government to direct or regulate the employment of capital, or enterprise, is mischievous. The only object of a wise Government should be, to remove obstructions to the free use of capital and industry. The politicians of Great Britain have become sensible of the truth of this position, and are receding from the system of arbitrary dictation and restrictions, and shall we now plunge into it? Shall we, at this time, put on the tattered garments of an exploded policy? . . .

The gentleman has called upon us to look at the petitions from every section of the country, and view the picture of general distress drawn up by the suffering citizens. Sir, I have examined these petitions, and have sought in vain for the picture of extreme distress which his warm imagination has painted. They state coolly and dispassionately, generally, that the great interests of the country are depressed; that industry does not receive the same liberal rewards as in former times; the manufacturers of the various articles of wool, cotton, iron, hemp, glass, &c., have stated the burdens and the pressure upon the particular articles, and appeal to the wisdom of Congress to provide some relief if practicable. But, sir, if gentlemen will examine these petitions, and the sources from which they come, they will find that those sections of our country which have most manufacturing

capital make the least complaint. Take, for instance, the six Eastern States, which, by the return of the amount of capital invested, or employed in manufactures in the several States, embraces about one-half of the whole amount employed in the whole country, while the population of these States comprises about one-sixth part of the whole population: from this whole section you do not find one-half as many petitions as from the State of New Jersey, or one-fourth as many as from Pennsylvania. Indeed, you find about as many remonstrating against your tariff bill, as of those who have appealed to your wisdom for relief, and very probably some of the same persons. After seeing the bill — for it does not appear probable that these petitioners ever expected such a remedy from the wisdom of Congress — where do you find a memorial praying Congress to impose additional duty on spirits and molasses? What petition can be found among the whole number, which asks you to change the great "leading policy," by compelling the people to change their occupations? What petition calls on Congress to sacrifice either agriculture or commerce for the support of manufactures? Where is the petition from the farmers, which asks you to impose additional duty on wheat? On hemp? On flax? Or even on wool? I believe there is one which asks for a duty on potatoes. But, sir, I understand the people of that State (Maine) are not much in favor of your tariff, nor are their Representatives among the strong supporters of this bill.

I ask the attention of the House to the bill itself. Let us examine its provisions, and see whether it is calculated to produce the effects contemplated by its advocates. It proposes a gradual increase of duty on manufactures of wool; but, in the next place, it proposes a higher rate of duty on the raw material — on the wool itself. This would operate as a bounty on the foreign manufacture, but for the minimum value of low-priced cloths; in fact, it will operate against the manufacture of fine cloth. But this duty on wool is for the benefit of agriculture and the consumer. I will not take up the time of the House in enumerating the many articles specified in the bill.

The next article I shall notice is *lead*. On this raw material you impose a tax of two cents per pound, for the benefit of the lead mines; and then on red and white lead manufactured from this raw material, four cents per pound, for the benefit of the manufacturer.

On hemp and flax, and on iron, you impose a duty in favor of agriculture; and on the manufacture of these articles a high duty, to protect the manufacturers. But here you seem to have forgotten the consumer — the ship, which is compelled to bear the burden of these double taxes, without any possible relief.

On mill cranks and mill irons, four cents per pound! I would ask whether this tax is for the benefit of the farmer, or the miller, or the man who eats the bread?

On almost every tool, by name, used by the mechanics, and on every implement used by the farmer — ploughs, hoes, scythes, spades, &c. — you impose heavy duties. Are these for the encouragement of agriculture or the mechanic arts? You propose even to tax heavily the cooking utensils used by the poor — the frying pans — but you have, in your great wisdom, struck out gridirons and griddles; whether because these are more generally in use among the rich, we have not been told.

On tallow, four cents per pound! This is to make fat beef and a good market for all the whale oil which can ever be collected. But, as it bears rather heavily on the tallow chandler and soap boiler, you allow a drawback on soap for his relief.

On indigo, alum, vitriol, copperas, and other articles used in manufacture, you propose a tax. We are bound to believe these are designed for the protection and encouragement of these manufactures....

Sir, in my opinion, your bill, like the Indian's description of *punch*, is made up of contradictions. The principles contained in it are at war with each other. You tax the implements of husbandry, and all the mechanic arts, to promote industry! You tax necessaries, instead of luxuries! You tax the raw material and the dyestuffs of your manufactures! You tax one man to support another, and then you tax the other to support him! You tax industry! You tax yourselves to support yourselves! You seem determined to bear your own burdens, and will not consent that others, who are willing, should assist you! In this way, you expect to grow rich and become independent! ...

George Holcombe of New York

... The bill, Mr. Speaker, is combatted on this floor by three interests essentially distinct; the agricultural interest of the South, the manufacturing interest of the East, and the general interest of commerce and navigation. For the sake of perspicuity, the objections arising out of the supposed hostility of the bill to each of these interests, will be noticed separately. The protection of the manufacturing interest is said to be hostile to the agriculture of the South. If gentlemen were able to establish the truth of this objection, the principles as well as the policy of the bill would remain, at least to me, entirely indefensible. For I have neither the right nor the disposition to advocate any measure calculated to build up the interest of one section of the Union at the expense of another. I have no personal interest which this bill can possibly promote. I support it, as a measure purely national in its character, intended to advance the prosperity, not of sections only, but of the Union; to equalize all our great interests; to promote, by its direct and necessary operation, the manufacturing interest; to promote, by the creation, or rather the extension, of the home market, the agricultural interest; and, finally, to promote the commercial interest, by enabling the American merchant, by the abundance and cheapness of the fabrics of the manufacturer, to adventure successfully in the great markets of the world; particularly in the opening and growing markets of South America.

The gentlemen of the South must pardon me for believing, as I certainly do believe, that they mistake altogether the ultimate operation of this bill, as far as their agriculture is concerned. It is true, we can only speculate upon this point. But it has always appeared to me that, if there be one section of the Union more deeply interested than another in the friendly operation of our manufacturing policy upon its agriculture, it must be the South, inasmuch as the creation of a steady home market for its rich agricultural staples must be to the South an object of vital and lasting consideration. The European market is at best precarious. A state of war impairs, and may extinguish it. Competition, also, seriously threatens it. The Southern planter, indeed, has already found in it growing and formidable rivals. Cotton, the great staple of the South, is at this moment extensively cultivated for exportation in three quarters of the globe, in India, Brazil, and, lately it would seem, in Egypt. And the time cannot be considered distant when it must form no inconsiderable staple of the whole series of South American Republics. Driven, therefore, as, in a great measure, it appears to me it necessarily must be driven, from the European market, where is the Southern planter to find refuge and protection, except, indeed, in the home market, which it is one of the first objects of this bill to assist in establishing? And a refuge and protection it assuredly will prove, ample and unchangeable, (the derision and infidelity of gentlemen to the contrary notwithstanding,) if we will consent to extend to it, from time to time, that legislative aid which its necessities may require, and which its great national importance will always justify. The American market, at present, consumes probably one-fourth, at least one-fifth, of all the cotton grown in the South; stimulated to excess as that culture has been by the extraordinary demands upon it, growing out of the peace of Europe. Extend, therefore, extend to the cotton manufacture of this country efficient protection, and I mistake, utterly and hopelessly mistake, the genius and enterprise engaged in it, if, before the revolution of another national period — the period of ten years — it be not able to absorb all the surplus cotton of the South, — for a part of Southern cotton, from its quality, will always find a market in Europe; provided, no more additional lands be appropriated to its culture; and the quantity is said already to trespass greatly upon correct agricultural proportions. . . .

But gentlemen contend that England

will refuse to purchase our cottons, if we refuse to purchase her fabrics. Mr. H. observed that this was no novel argument, but one which had been repeatedly urged in Congress, and also in the reviews and essays of the day. He denounced it; and particularly the principle upon which it is founded, as offensive and fallacious. And what, Mr. Speaker, is this principle? It is, that we, the guardians and protectors of the rights and interests of the good people of these States, should look calmly on, whilst our infant manufactures perish before us; or, that we should see them struggling into existence, unnoticed, unaided, and unprotected. That we should consent to postpone indefinitely one of our greatest interests, and subscribe, officially, to articles of virtual and lasting dependence upon foreign nations! For what? To protect the cotton culture of the South from imaginary extinction! Or rather, which is really in fact, to give to the English manufacturer the monopoly of the American market forever.

But the proposition which is assumed, that England will refuse to purchase our cottons if we refuse to purchase her fabrics, is wholly gratuitous. Long before this Government first manifested any serious disposition to foster the manufacturing interest, cotton had been extensively imported into England from India and Brazil, and its culture in those places sedulously encouraged. The English manufacturer purchases from the cheapest market, (can we suppose he can or will pursue for any length of time any other course?) entirely regardless of the country that grows it. It is true, the prices being alike, and the quality the same, he will purchase the cottons of every other country in preference to ours. And the cause is obvious. He has foreseen, from our uncommon skill as manufacturers, and the extraordinary progress which we

have already made in every department of useful industry, that the time is not distant when the monopoly which he enjoys upon these shores will not only be extinguished, but rivals will here grow up to compete, with him, in all the great markets of the world. And hence his disposition to promote, in preference to ours, the agriculture of every nation, where new markets can be created. And this is the course which he will pursue – this indeed is the course which he must pursue – in despite of every effort of conciliation – of every act of favoritism which we may be disposed to extend towards him. As long as we continue to undersell the foreign agriculturist in the European market we shall be preferred – but certainly no longer. Every other consideration is idle – is but dust in the balance when weighed against this obvious, this irresistible fact.

But this bill, Mr. Speaker, is further said to be hostile to the general agricultural interest of this country. I must pass over very rapidly an objection so decisively extravagant. For where in the history of the world has the encouragement of manufactures ever proved hostile to the interests of agriculture? Look to the present age – go to the Lothians of Scotland; the rich agricultural districts of England; the kingdom of the Netherlands; the banks of the Rhine and the Elbe; the Rhone and the Seine; go indeed to every manufacturing hamlet, circle or city in Europe, and witness everywhere the refutation of this extravagant objection. Ask history – summon from the dead the Saracens of Spain, the Lombards of the twelfth century – the Genoese; the Venetian – ask the illustrious house of Medicis whether the fostering care which they awarded to manufactures proved hostile to the agriculture of the beautiful region over which they presided? Even our own short experience amply refutes the objection.

Wherever manufacturing establishments have been successfully located amongst us, the country has, in all instances, flourished around them — exhibiting the strongest evidence of their friendly influence upon the interests of the farmer. And were we disposed to receive, with due courtesy, the representations of our constituents, our tables at this moment would be covered with memorials from our agricultural constituents — at least from those of the middle States and the East and the West, praying for the protection of the manufacturer — experience having dissipated their early hostilities, and convinced them, by the most irresistible testimony, that in the protection of the manufacturer is embraced their own surest and best protection.

But the bill, Mr. Speaker, is said to be hostile to the interests of commerce. This, if sustained, would prove an argument entirely unanswerable. Inasmuch as it would not only render a resort to excises or direct taxation necessary to meet the ordinary expenditures of the Government, but involves seriously and lastingly the interests of the Navy. Mr. H. controverted this argument at some length. He maintained that it was opposed by the testimony of innumerable facts, and the universal experience of the commercial world — that commerce is directly promoted by whatever tends to promote national wealth and industry. That the bill, in its present shape, was as judicious a revision of the tariff as could be devised; and, consequently, that the interests of commerce and the revenue, instead of being impaired, would be promptly and decisively promoted by it. That domestic manufactures create a multitude of new wants, and furnish the means of gratifying them; and hence, consumption is increased; and

hence, the loss which the revenue sustains by the lessened importation of articles manufactured at home, is more than repaired by the increased consumption of others; and that, if to these considerations be added the steady and extraordinary advance of our population, and the necessary increase of luxury, the interests of the revenue may be fairly regarded, as secure from all future contingency and danger. As a striking illustration of the above positions, Mr. H. referred to the example of England, whose revenue has constantly increased, exactly in proportion as the restrictive system, for the encouragement of the manufacturing interest, has been enforced. Mr. H. contended further, that a more rigid tariff than the present — a tariff for the ample and exclusive protection of the great objects of our industry, would, whatever might be its immediate operation, ultimately advance (and at no distant period too) the interest of commerce. Such a tariff, it is acknowledged, would extinguish some of the fountains of commerce — but open a four-fold number in their stead. . . .

But this bill, sir, has excited the hostility of the manufacturing interest itself, particularly of the flourishing manufacturing interest in the East. A single remark, in reply to this objection. This hostility, ungenerous and unbecoming as it may seem, is perfectly natural. The manufacturer has perceived, (and certainly the perception required no preternatural illumination,) that the ultimate operation of this bill, by bringing additional skill, capital, and competition into the business, will tend to lessen, rather than multiply, his profits. And hence his hostility. A fact worth a thousand speculations, urged, as they may be, with all the zeal and perseverance of the gentlemen of the South. Do not gentlemen perceive the dilemma to which this argument reduces them? The South combats the bill, because it will advance the price of goods, and thus operate as a permanent and oppressive tax upon its agriculture. The manufacturing interest of the East, on the contrary, combats it, because it will destroy monopoly, and reduce the price of the manufactured article below its present value, to the minimum of a living profit. . . .

But, what kind of tariff would gentlemen be willing to tolerate? What, I repeat, is the nature of the commercial system which they are disposed to establish as the permanent policy of this country? It is something which I can scarcely comprehend, and certainly not define. Something, I presume, graduated to the minimum of an ordinary revenue law, and based upon the principle of Adam Smith, that national prosperity is best promoted by an entire dissolution of commercial restrictions — by a free and liberal intercourse among nations. Come, then, let us test for a moment this specious, captivating theory. Let us pursue this free, this liberal system, to its legitimate, its ultimate consequences. Repeal your revenue laws; raze your custom-houses to their foundations; give your commercial restrictions, of every description, to the winds; and, after you have achieved these triumphs over the institutions — the delusions, if you please, of ages — go reap the golden, glorious harvest which awaits you. Alas! you have sown in the winds and must reap the desolation of the whirlwind. The Kalmuc of the Crimea will supply you with bread; the Copt of Egypt, and the Indian of Bengal with cotton; England, as formerly, with your household furniture, and France with the articles of your wardrobe. Your great interests paralyzed; your agriculture languishing; commerce declining; manufactures perishing; your — But, sir, I cannot, will not finish the picture. It is too utterly repulsive and extravagant. But, repulsive as it is, and extravagant as it may seem to be, it is a picture faithfully correct, and exhibits, in strong relief, the desolation and extremity to which the favorite system of gentlemen opposed to this tariff — the system of unrestricted commerce, in the present state of the world, if adopted and persevered in, would necessarily and rapidly reduce us. . . .

George McDuffie of South Carolina

. . . On this question, if I may be permitted, and I scarcely know whether I ought to venture upon it, I will lay down a general principle, upon the authority of Adam Smith, who, notwithstanding the terms of sweeping condemnation which have been applied to his speculations, has done more to enlighten the world on the science of political economy than any man of modern times. He is the founder of the science. All that has been since done is but a development or modification of the principles he established. What, then, is his great elementary principle? That labor and capital, if left to receive their direction from individual sagacity, will naturally seek, and speedily find, the most profitable employments. And this is founded upon the idea that individuals are more capable of forming a judgment as to what will promote their pecuniary interests, than the most enlightened Gov-

Annals of Congress, ibid., April 16, 1824, pp. 2403–2426.

ernment can possibly be, from the very nature of things. This, however, is denounced as empty theory! . . . Shall we undertake to enlighten the capitalists of Boston as to the most profitable mode of investing their disengaged capital? They would laugh to scorn the folly and impotence of such officious dictation. It will scarcely be alleged that our people have not a taste for the products of manufacture. For all the productions of human industry — for all the articles, at least, of which we propose to encourage the domestic fabrication, the people of this country have perhaps too keen an appetite. Indeed, the complaint of the friends of this measure is, that they import them in too great abundance. No legislation, therefore, is necessary to create a demand for those articles. In such a state of things, the general principle is indisputably true, that capital and labor will naturally flow into the most profitable channels of industry, without the control of Government.

But, to this general principle I admit there is an exception, which I will candidly state. . . . But the principal ground upon which the protecting policy can in any case be justified, is the inability of infant manufacturing establishments to sustain a successful competition with their foreign rivals, even after the country has reached the point at which the domestic article can, with the experience of a few years, be fabricated cheaper than the foreign. And here, sir, the limit of the protecting system is distinctly indicated. It must be satisfactorily shown, that the protection sought is only temporary; and that, after a reasonable time is given to acquire experience and skill, and bring the domestic manufactories to perfection, they can furnish the domestic fabrics cheaper than similar fabrics could be obtained from abroad. Now, if we apply these principles to the actual protection

heretofore extended to our domestic manufactures, it will be seen that the Government has already fulfilled its obligations to them, in the amplest manner. Gentlemen have argued this question as if the manufacturing interest of the country had been unjustly assailed by some foreign power, and Congress had manifested the most cruel indifference to their sufferings. But is there the slightest foundation for either of these assumptions? The only power with which our manufacturers have had permanently to contend, is the superior natural advantages of the foreign artisan; and I will now call the attention of the House to the protection which our establishments have actually received from this Government. I venture to assert, that since the commencement of the restrictive system in 1807, the manufacturers of this country have enjoyed an unusual and artificial stimulus from our legislation; and I am perfectly satisfied that it is this extraordinary stimulus that has given them that voracious appetite for prohibition which nothing, it seems, but the absolute protection of all rival articles can satiate.

. . . But the measure which gave the strongest impulse to our manufactures, was the war of 1812. And here it is worth remarking, that a war with England gives a stimulus to manufactures, which no other kind of protection can possibly afford. For, at the same time that it cuts off our trade with the nation that principally supplies us with manufactures, it compensates the diminished consumption of them by the people, by the extraordinary consumption of the Government. At the close of the war, the system of double duties was continued till 1816, when the existing tariff was enacted for the avowed purpose of sustaining those establishments which the war had brought into existence, against the extraordinary influx of foreign manufactures, resulting from the universal restoration of peace in Europe. . . .

It is obvious, then, that the protection of these establishments, which originated in the war, is not the object of the present bill. It does not even assume this modesty of pretension. Doctrines are now advanced, which never entered into the conception of those who advocated the tariff of 1816 – doctrines which, though maintained by gentlemen who have waged a special war of sneers and sarcasms against the theories of political economy, throw into the shade the boldest theories of the French economists. We are now told that it is the duty of a paternal Government not only to protect existing interests against extraordinary reverses which it has contributed to produce, but to create new manufactures and new pursuits, by the mere energy of legislation. The people, it is said, are absolutely idle and in wretchedness, for the want of employment. . . .

. . . Shall we be told, in a country like this, abounding with almost interminable wilds of fertile lands, that a tithe of the people are suffering for the want of something to do? Sir, there are innumerable avenues to employment in this country, and if any man were to make his complaint to me that he was without employment, I could tell him simply *to go to work*. That is the obvious remedy, a remedy in the reach of every one; and, if it were more generally pursued, there must soon be an end of this wretched and delusive dependence upon the quackery of legislation for employment. Sir, I boldly assert that there is not a single individual in the vast extent of this Republic, that cannot readily obtain, not only employment, but such an employment as will enable him to improve his condition. This is the only country on earth where a common laborer, of industry and enterprise, can, in the course of an ordinary lifetime, besides comfortably supporting himself and his family, leave to his children an inheritance of real estate: and, with these facts staring us in the face, we are required to believe, on the authority of tabular statements, that the people can only be saved from suffering and discontent, by the adoption of this measure, to provide them with employment. The gentleman from New York, by way of confirming his general conclusion, has stated that the wages of a laborer in his vicinity, is only twelve and a half cents a day. In answer to this, I can only say to the gentleman, that, if his distressed neighbors will only make a transition from Long Island to any other point in the whole Union, even the most unfavorable, I will be responsible for their obtaining fifty cents per day. . . .

I will now take the liberty of addressing a few words especially to the Representatives of the West, on the subject of their own interests. A subject upon which I certainly will not presume to instruct them. But I am sure they will excuse a friendly admonition, when I state the particular topic to which it relates. I am well assured that the permanent prosperity of the West depends more upon the improvement of the means of transporting their produce to market, and of receiving the returns, than upon every other subject to which the legislation of this Government can be directed. . . .

I will also present another view of certain interests of the West, which are intimately connected with the portion of the country I have the honor to represent.

Gentlemen are aware that a very profitable trade is carried on by their constituents with the Southern country, in live stock of all descriptions, which they drive over the mountains and sell for cash. This extensive trade, which, from its peculiar character, more easily overcomes the difficulties of transportation than any that can be substituted in its place, is about to be put in jeopardy for the conjectural benefits of this measure. When I say this trade is about to be put in jeopardy, I do not speak inadvisedly. I am perfectly convinced, that, if this bill passes, it will have the effect of inducing the people of the South, partly from the feeling, and partly from the necessity growing out of it, to raise within themselves, the live stock which they now purchase from the West. It is at least certain that more will be lost in this trade, than is gained in that of cotton bagging. . . .

. . . When it is urged that too much of our capital and labor are applied to agricultural pursuits, and that we ought to encourage manufactures, because we have not a due proportion of our industry devoted to that essential branch of national wealth; though I believe that existing laws and the natural course of things, will afford all the encouragement that ought to be desired; yet I can understand the argument. It is not only intelligible, but plausible. But when it is contended that we must protect and encourage, by duties on rival productions, not only manufacturing industry, of which it is alleged we have too little, but agricultural, of which we have too much, I confess myself utterly at a loss to comprehend what is the practical end at which gentlemen are aiming. But, whatever may be their aim, it is certain that the result of their system would be the destruction of commerce. If we make everything we consume at home, we will, of course, import nothing; and if we import nothing, it is a self-evident proposition that we can export nothing. . . .

Now, the professed object of this measure is to provide a substitute for foreign manufactures, and thereby prevent their importation. Is it not self-evident, then, that you will diminish our existing commerce precisely to the extent that you augment your domestic manufactures? But this wonder-working bill, it seems, is to furnish a substitute for those branches of our foreign commerce that it will destroy. If any thing, on such a subject, is susceptible of demonstration, I think it is the delusiveness of such an expectation. Of what, I ask, is this new commerce to consist? It will be at once perceived that it cannot exist without new articles, both of exportation and importation. What, then, shall we be enabled to export that we do not now? Manufactures, it is said. But, can it be seriously contended that manufactures, which cannot hold a competition with the foreign in our own markets, with the heavy duties which have existed for the last eight years, but require the additional protection provided in this bill, can maintain a successful competition in foreign markets? In other words, when, with an average protection (including duties and transportation) of at least thirty per cent., we cannot command the home market, how is it possible that we can command the foreign markets, in which we shall have no such protection? I do pronounce it to be absolutely a visionary expectation. For at least half a century to come, the British manufacturers will exclude us from foreign markets. A few occasional exceptions, resulting from peculiar circumstances, do not weaken the general proposition.

But, another inquiry remains to be made in relation to the commerce which is to compensate for that which we destroy. What description of articles shall we import in this new commerce? It cannot be manufactures, for our policy excludes these of course. They are to be our exports under this new system. What, then, shall we import? The productions of the soil? These, we are told, are super-abundant, and literally rotting on our hands for the want of a market. This new commerce, then, is to realize the splendid but empty vision of exporting every thing and importing nothing! By such a commerce, we should certainly avoid one evil which haunts the imaginations of some gentlemen: The balance of trade would never be against us. But, sir, let us examine this subject a little more minutely. It is said we shall export our manufactures to South America. There we shall come in competition with British manufactures. Admitting, for a moment, that we could sell our manufactures as cheap as the British could sell theirs in the markets of South America, yet we should be excluded, because that country produces nothing that we want, but precisely that which our rivals want. The great staple of South America will be unmanufactured cotton, which is the great staple of this country also. And nothing can be more idle than to calculate upon a profitable commerce, or, indeed, any commerce at all, between two countries that produce precisely the same articles for exportation. The argument, therefore, that our commerce will not be diminished by this system, is, in my judgment, utterly fallacious. And even if it were true, in point of fact, that a new commerce could be substituted for that which we cut off, it would only be giving up a natural and profitable, for a forced and unprofitable trade. And here I will remark that there seems to be a palpable inconsistency in the arguments of the advocates of this measure. They tell us, in one breath, that their object is to relieve the country from its dependence on foreign commerce, and in the next, that our foreign commerce will be increased. If this latter proposition be true, our dependence on foreign commerce will be

greater under the proposed system than it now is. And, unless it can be shown that this measure will produce two opposite and inconsistent effects at the same time, it will be difficult to make out the proposition that our commerce will be increased, and our dependence on commerce diminished. . . .

Looking to the operation of this measure upon the different classes of the community, it may be fairly stated as its general result, that it will sacrifice the laboring classes for the benefit of the capitalists. And when I say capitalists, I include as well those who employ capital in some of the products of agriculture, as in manufactures. You propose to protect, by duties, not only manufactures, but wool, hemp, and even grain. Ridiculous as the duty upon this last article is, it serves admirably to illustrate the genius of the system.

Although the manufacturing interest makes the most prominent figure in this scheme of protection, the question is no longer between the manufacturing and agricultural interests, but between all those who produce more than they consume of the articles subject to duty, and those who purchase that surplus production. From this it is obvious, that but a very small part of the community can enjoy the benefit of this system, which operates as a permanent tax upon the remainder. As to the manufacturers we know their number is exceedingly small in comparison with the aggregate of our population. But the smallness of the number of farmers who can be benefited by this bill, is not so obvious. There exists a delusion on this point, which is easily removed. It is supposed that the great mass of the farmers will participate in the bounties provided. But every practical observer must know, in relation to wool, for example, that a great majority of the farmers can produce no more than they consume in their own families. It will be the more wealthy farmers, therefore, who will realize the advantages, such as they may be, of this compromise with the manufacturers, while the small farmers and the whole class of mere laborers will be compelled to bear the burdens of the system, such as they certainly are, without the slightest equivalent. No man has pretended, no man will venture to assert, that the price of labor will be increased by this measure. That, sir, the thing which most deserves encouragement, is left unbountied to its fate. I do pronounce it, that this is a combination, not only of the few against the many, but of the wealthy against the poor; we take from those who have not, and give to those who have. I speak with studied precision when I say, that those who consume what they do not make, are taxed for the benefit of those who make what they do not consume. These are the true antagonist powers of this system. . . .

. . . I stated, and I now deliberately repeat it, that the cotton of the Southern States, the great source of our prosperity, constituting one-third of the whole export of the Union, has reached that critical point in the competition with foreign cottons, when any material derangement of our commercial relations with Great Britain must inevitably expose us to the hazard of losing the market of that country, at least to a very considerable extent. If we cease to take the manufactures of Great Britain, she will assuredly cease to take our cotton to the same extent. It is settled principle of her policy — a principle not only wise but essential to her existence — to purchase from those nations who receive her manufactures, in preference to those who do not. You have, heretofore, been her best customers, and therefore it has been her policy to purchase our cotton to the full extent of our demand for her manufactures. But, say gentlemen, Great Britain does not purchase our cotton from affection, but interest. I grant it sir, and that is the very reason of my decided hostility to a system which will make it her interest to purchase from other countries than our own. It is her interest to purchase cotton, even at a higher price, from those countries which receive her manufactures in exchange. It is better for her to give a little more for cotton, than to obtain nothing for her manufactures. It will be remarked, that the situation of Great Britain is, in this respect, widely different from that of the United States. The powers of her soil have been already pushed very nearly to the maximum of their productiveness. The productiveness of her manufactures, on the contrary, is as unlimited as the demand of the whole world. She, therefore, has no choice of pursuits. Her surplus capital and labor must be directed to manufactures, or remain idle and unproductive. A demand for her manufactures is, then, from the very necessity of her condition, the primary consideration, to which every other must be subservient in the regulation of her commercial relations. To say, therefore, that she will continue to purchase our cotton, because she can get it a little cheaper than other cottons, after we have ceased to purchase her manufactures, is to suppose that she will be utterly blind to her own necessities; that she will, in fact, abandon, where it is most indispensable, that very policy which the friends of this bill now call upon us to adopt, in a spirit of reckless speculation, without considering that our circumstances are the very reverse of those which render such a policy necessary to Great Britain. In fact, sir, the policy of Great Britain is not, as gentlemen seem to suppose, to secure the *home* but the *foreign* market for her manufactures. The former she has without an effort. It is to attain the latter that all her policy and enterprise are brought into requisition. The manufactures of that country are the basis of her commerce; our manufactures, on the contrary, are to be the destruction of our commerce. And yet, in a spirit of blind and undiscriminating imitation, we are called upon to follow the example of Great Britain, by adopting a policy which will produce a result precisely the opposite of that which she has experienced of her policy; or, in other words, we are required to adopt, in deference to British wisdom, a system the very reverse of that which British policy would pursue, under the same circumstances! . . .

George McDuffie of South Carolina

. . . What, then, let us briefly inquire, is the tendency, and what has been the effect, of the high duties imposed for the purpose of protecting manufactures and other domestic productions? It is too plain to admit of argument: indeed, it has been candidly admitted by the chairman of the Committee on Manufactures, in former discussions, that domestic productions can only be protected by prohibiting the foreign articles that would come in competition with them. He openly avowed that he aimed at prohibition, and it would have been folly to have aimed at less, if he really meant to give protection. No duty can give any protection to any domestic fabric, which does not exclude a similar foreign fabric; and, in the very nature of things, the amount of protection cannot exceed the amount of prohibition, though it may, and generally does, fall short of it. You cannot create a demand, for example, for any domestic manufacture, by legislation, otherwise than by excluding a similar foreign manufacture; and as your legislation is calculated to enhance the price of the article, you certainly cannot create by it a demand for a greater amount of the domestic fabric than you exclude of the foreign. It may be confidently assumed, therefore, that whatever may be the amount of iron and salt, and manufactures of cotton, wool, iron, and hemp, which have been brought into existence in the United States by the system of high protecting duties, at least an equal amount of foreign rival productions has been excluded by those duties. It will not be deemed an extravagant estimate to suppose that the protecting system has caused to be produced, annually, articles of these various kinds, to the amount of twelve millions of dollars, which would not have been produced, but for the protection given them. It follows, then, as a corollary, that at least an equal amount of these articles of foreign production must have been excluded. But these are the very articles which we receive from Great Britain, France, and Holland, in exchange for our agricultural staples. By excluding twelve millions of such articles, therefore, we necessarily diminish the foreign demand for our staples, and principally cotton, to that amount. There is scarcely any limit to the consumption of our cotton in Europe, but that which is imposed by

Congressional Debates, 21 Congress, 1 session (Washington: Gales & Seaton, 1830), VI, April 29, 1830, pp. 850–860.

our refusal to take manufactures in exchange for it. If, therefore, we were permitted to import the twelve millions of dollars worth of manufactures that have been excluded by our commercial restrictions, or, rather, if they had never been excluded by those restrictions, it cannot be reasonably doubted that we should now have a demand in Europe for four hundred thousand bales of cotton, beyond the existing demand. Even, therefore, if we grant, what is not the fact, that the whole of the domestic demand for cotton has been produced by the prohibitory effect of our tariff, it will follow that we have gained a market for one hundred and fifty thousand bales, by sacrificing one for four hundred thousand. From this estimate, it will be seen that the prohibition of foreign imports has resulted in curtailing the entire demand for cotton in the markets of the whole world, including our own, two hundred and fifty thousand bales. In addition, then, to the annual burden he bears in paying the duties upon the imports he is still permitted to bring into the country, the planter sustains an annual loss of seven million five hundred thousand dollars, being the value of the cotton for which he has lost a market, in consequence of the unjust restrictions imposed upon his lawful commerce by the suicidal policy of his own Government. . . .

The great misfortune is, sir — and it gives us the true key to this whole system — that, while this Government is an undivided and indivisible unity, the country over which it extends is divided into various and — disguise it as we may — diametrically adverse interests. Hence, it results, that the law which throws a restriction upon the commerce of the southern States, to the great and obvious injury of the planter, is obviously calculated, and professedly intended, to promote the interest of the northern manufacturer. If the manufacturer can gain ten per cent. by the restriction, it is his interest to adhere to it, though it impose a burden of forty or fifty per cent. upon the planter. Hence it is that the majority of this House are pursuing a policy with regard to the interests of the whole Union, which no human being would pursue in regard to his own interest. It is worth while, sir, to trace the operation of this policy a little more in detail. Great Britain, it is alleged, will not, or, which is the same thing, does not, in fact, purchase the grain of the northern, middle, and western States, and, consequently, those States have nothing wherewith to purchase British manufactures. This is the complaint. Now, sir, if this be true, the wisdom of man could not more effectually exclude British manufactures, or give a more complete protection to domestic manufactures, in those States. If they have nothing to give in exchange for British manufactures, what earthly necessity is there to exclude them by law? The domestic manufacturer is absolutely secured against foreign competition by the single fact, that the British manufacturer will not take any thing in exchange for his fabrics, which the people of those States have to give. What, then, is the real object of the restrictions which the tariff States are so anxious to throw about our foreign commerce? It is not, sir, be assured, to prevent those States from importing British manufactures, who have nothing to give in exchange for them. That would be impotent and gratuitous legislation. The true object — disguise it as gentlemen may — is to prevent those States who have the means of paying for British manufactures, and who have a deep and vital interest in preserving that branch of commerce, from importing those manufactures, in order to promote the interest of those States who have not the means of paying for British manufactures, and who really have, or believe they have, a deep and vital interest in destroying that branch of commerce. Twist it and turn it as you may, "to this complexion it must come at last." Hence it is, that to the gross inequality of the revenue system of the United States, the majority of Congress have superadded the intolerable burdens of the prohibitory system. Will any gentleman from Massachusetts, or Rhode Island, or Vermont, have the hardihood to maintain that the duties imposed on cotton and woollen manufactures, varying from forty to sixty per cent. are equally a burden upon his constituents as they are upon mine? Will any gentleman from Pennsylvania assert that the enormous duty upon iron imposes an equal burden upon the people of Pennsylvania and upon those of South Carolina? On the contrary, do not these gentlemen distinctly and openly avow that the duties which throw a grievous and oppressive burden upon the people of the southern States, operate as a beneficial and sustaining bounty to the people of the northern and eastern States? I do firmly believe, that, if the proceeds of the public lands would defray the whole expenses of the Government, or if the staple-growing States would assume the responsibility of paying those expenses out of revenues raised by themselves, there are certain States in this Union — I allude to those emphatically denominated tariff States — that would not consent to a repeal of the impost duties. No, sir, they gain much more than they lose, by the aggregate effect of the duties imposed, and the disbursements made, by this Government, regarding the system in the light of a mere pecuniary speculation. If a foreign invention were made, by which the operations of Government could be carried on without the expenditure of a single dollar, those States would regard it as a nuisance, and prohibit its importation by as rigorous penalties as are now proposed in regard to foreign manufactures. A greater calamity could scarcely happen to the interests of northern capital, confederated in favor of the protecting system, than would result from an entire suspension of the fiscal operations of this Government, including both taxation and disbursement. . . .

The representatives of the manufacturing and tariff States allege that they have large and extensive manufacturing establishments, which it is their interest and their right to encourage and protect, and deny the right of the southern representatives to interfere with their protecting policy. Now, sir, as a southern representative, I claim no right to interfere with any protection, which any portion of the northern States may choose to extend, at their own expense, to their own manufactories. All I pretend to claim, is the right to put my veto upon this scheme of injustice and plunder, by which the property, the rightful and exclusive property, of my constituents, is unconstitutionally applied to that object.

There cannot be a proposition more self-evidently just and equitable, than that those States in which the manufacturing establishments are situated, should bear the burden of protecting them. Can a man be found, sir, in this House, or out of it, who would have the boldness to contest this position? Then why do not the manufacturing States protect their own manufactures? Will it be pretended that they have not the constitutional power? Has not the Legislature of every State in the Union an unlimited power to impose taxes upon the people of the State, and appropriate the proceeds, in the form of bounties, for the protection of domestic manufactures, or any other branch of domestic industry? No man of common information — no man, indeed, of common sense, will deny that every State Legislature has this power. Why, then, is it not exercised? Is the protection it would afford less direct and efficient than that which is afforded by the imposition of high impost duties? I will answer this question in the language of a man to whom the manufacturers have always looked, as to an oracle — I mean Alexander Hamilton. Speaking of "pecuniary bounties," he says: "This has been found one of the most efficacious means of encouraging manufactures; it is in some views the best.

"It is a species of encouragement more positive and direct than any other, and, for that very reason, has a more immediate tendency to stimulate and uphold new enterprises. . . ."

. . . How, then, has it come to pass, that, while the manufacturers have been, for more than ten years past, clamoring at our doors for protection, the Legislature of no single State in the Union, so far as I am informed, has ever appropriated a cent, or raised a finger, to sustain these languishing and suffering interests, which certainly have a claim upon the States for protection, if indeed they have any claim at all? Sir, I have frequently put this question in former discussions upon this floor, and have never found a man bold enough to answer it. The advocates of the protecting system have invariably passed it over with a prudent and profound silence. The reason is obvious. No man dare to avow openly the true cause why the manufacturing States, having the undoubted power, will not extend any protection to their own manufacturers, but send them to Congress for relief.

The moral sense of this nation would not tolerate the avowal, that the State of Massachusetts, for example, will not tax her own citizens to afford protection to her own manufactures, because the Federal Government can be made the unrighteous instrument of taxing the people of the southern States for the purpose of affording that protection.

This, sir, disguise it as gentlemen may, is the true question involved in the protecting system. The tariff States would permit every establishment within their limits to sink into utter ruin, before they would levy taxes from their own citizens to nourish and sustain them. That would be too plain and palpable a proceeding. It would instantly open the eyes of the people to the true character of the protecting system. It would tear off from the monster the veil which conceals its horrible deformity, and break its infatuating charm forever. If the protection afforded to the manufacturers by this Government were entirely withdrawn to-morrow, I do not believe there is a State Legislature in the Union, that would dare to substitute an equivalent protection in the form of pecuniary bounties drawn from the people of the State, and appropriated from the public treasury. Nothing that could be possibly suggested, in the way of argument, would exhibit the palpable injustice of this system in so strong a light as the course pursued, in this respect, by the Legislatures of the tariff States. Would any man believe, sir, that the Legislature of a sovereign State would memorialize Congress to protect the manufactures of that State, by imposing restrictions and duties upon the commerce of other States, when that Legislature, having the admitted power to protect those manufactures, utterly neglects to do it? Yet such was the conduct of the Legislature of Massachusetts; and such is, substantially, the course pursued by the Legislatures of all the tariff States. . . .

The southern States, then, are reduced to the very same relation to the tariff States, in point of principle, as that in which all the colonies formerly stood to Great Britain. They have changed their masters, to be sure; and I will now proceed to inquire what they have gained by the change.

I confidently assert that the restrictions imposed by the tariff States upon the commerce of the planting States, are one hundred times more injurious and oppressive than all the colonial restrictions and taxes which Great Britain ever imposed, or attempted to impose, upon the commerce of our forefathers. Yes, sir, a revolution which severed a mighty empire into fragments, and which history has already recorded as the first in the annals of human liberty, originated in restrictions and impositions, not a whit more tyrannical in principle, and, as I will proceed to demonstrate, not a hundredth part so oppressive in point of fact, as the restrictions and impositions now unconstitutionally imposed upon the southern States.

III   EDITORIAL OPINION

Hezekiah Niles, editor and printer of Niles' Weekly Register

The "Prohibitory System"

THE "PROHIBITORY SYSTEM." The *farmers* of the United States, seeking the establishment of a sure market at home for the surplus productions of their *own soil*, planted by their *own hands* and gathered with the sweat of their *own brow*, through the agency of *domestic manufactures*, are held up as a class of persons aiming at a "MONOPOLY," and as desiring "prohibitory laws," by the very men who *possess* and *enjoy*, and *profit* by, *all, and every, prohibitory law that has been, or is, inserted as a permanent measure in the statutes of our country!* There is a degree of assurance — perhaps, it would be right to call it impudence, in this, that would make one laugh, if laugh one could, at a matter so seriously interesting to those who have to bear the "burthen and the heat of the day," in war and in peace. That it is the *farmers,* and not a "few manufacturers" who are seeking a protective tariff, is indisputable.

The *cuckoo* cry about "monopoly" has been suffered to go on so long, that those who use it seem to have acquired just as much *right* to it as the "holy" conspirators at Verona thought they possessed to regulate the affairs of Spain — to restore a poor fool to absolute power, and place a gallant people in chains; re-establish the *infernal* inquisition by pretensions to religion, and promote the mild doctrines of the SAVIOUR by a deluge of the blood of men! I intend to speak plainly, and deal in palpable facts. I will shew that the farmers seek only a small share of that *protection* which is really extended to their severest opponents, and that the latter are conditioned like a flying culprit who joins in the shout of "stop thief!" to save himself from arrest — but I hope to secure them and bring them to *judgment* before "the bar of the public reason," to be dealt with according to their deserts. We shall see "how a plain table will put them down."

But first, it may be well to ascertain the meaning of the word "monopoly"— it is said to be "an engrossing of commodities." In a free country and among a free people, with equality of rights and condition, it is impossible that *the majority* can be monopolizers; or, if even so, it would be proper, because the majority, by the laws of "nature and nature's GOD," should rule. But monopoly means the grasping of the few at the expense of the many — and such is the operation of it among us; all monopoly, *if monopoly there is*, being unquestionably with a small minority. Take the broadest ground possible as shewn by the votes of the representatives of the people on the tariff bill in 1818, and it will appear that *five* millions (of citizens) were in favor and *three* millions against that measure; and, by the assessment lists and the census, it is easy to shew that the former possessed *much more* than twice the disposable strength and solid wealth of the latter, which, nevertheless, defeated the passage of the law, and so still secured for their own benefit every thing like a "monopoly" in the United States, or maintained the *exclusive* advantages derivable from the "prohibitory laws" of the nation. I am quite willing to admit, that the greater part of this minority acted conscientiously; but I think I almost know that with some of them it was a mere matter of *dollars* and *cents,* as their own pockets might be affected. They had accomplished all that they desired for their own profit, and then they combined with others to deny to a majority of their fellow citizens a *common protection with themselves!* Here is the spirit of trade, that, as I have before said, "would enter into contract with Satan, to supply his dominions with fuel." But for my part, I regard all men as BAD MEN, who claim for themselves any liberty or advantage which they refuse to others, equally entitled to enjoy or possess it as the property of all.

The only laws of the United States which were really intended to be *prohibitory* in their operation, are those that relate to *tonnage,* the *coasting trade,* the *fisheries,* and *coarse cotton goods* — all which came from the east, were opposed by the south, but carried through the liberality of the people of the middle states, for the general reason that domestic industry ought to be encouraged, as indispensable to the progress of the national prosperity. We shall see what their generous acts, (especially the three first), have cost us, and what return of courtesy has been rendered for them. . . .

Let us add up and ascertain what the "protection of commerce" and the encouragement of the fisheries, &c. have cost us, or lost to the treasury —THAT being the centre point of the "notions" of those who speak of "monopolies" and "prohibitions"— but it is not mine.

1. The allowances (or bounty) on the fisheries, since the establishment of the government, have actually cost, deducting the duty on the salt used in curing fish exported, two or three millions.

2. The difference between the duties on merchandize and tonnage that would have been paid, had all the foreign goods used by us been imported in foreign vessels, is at least equal to fifty millions, for the same time.

3. The "monopoly" of the coasting trade may be estimated at not less than fifteen millions.

4. The navy built for the "protection of commerce," cost about 27 millions up to the period of the late war, and *then* it was *first regarded as an arm of the national defence*. Charge only *one half* its cost since to *commerce*, which is very reasonable, considering the fleets that we have kept up in the Mediterranean and the West Indies, and the ships sent to the South Seas; thus the aggregate expense of the *protection* afforded by the navy, will be about fifty-two millions of dollars.

5. Our ministers to foreign countries, with which, in general, we have no sort of business, except such as relates to *commerce*, have, variously, cost us about a million and an half — say one million to "protect commerce."

RECAPITULATION

Allowances on the fisheries	$ 2,500,000
Difference on duties and tonnage	50,000,000
"Monopoly" of the coasting trade	15,000,000
The navy	52,000,000
Foreign ministers	1,000,000
	$120,500,000

To this may justly be added the whole cost of the late war, for that was purely a commercial affair. It is morally certain, that we should not have been involved in it, but on account of the shipping interest, whose conduct therein we cannot forget, though it is not pleasant to memory.

Now, though the protection of commerce has cost the people of the United States, or kept out of the treasury, (according to the present wise mode of calculation), a far greater sum than I have put down, — I am prepared to say that the cost, or loss, was infinitely advantageous to the people at large. It employed, to fall and hew timber in the forest and transport it to navigable waters, in persons to build and fit ships and vessels and in the navigation of them, in raising food

and other supplies for their subsistence, in merchants, waggoners, carters and draymen, &c. not less than two hundred thousand able bodied, productive and invaluable men, on whom depended the subsistence, of about or not less than four hundred thousand other persons — their wives and children; and all these were supported in comfort, who might, otherwise, and without such employment, have hung as dead weights on the community, or, at least, been miserable. There is *many times* a greater number, directly or indirectly, employed or supported by the manufactory of articles, and in the subsistence of those employed in the manner just stated; but they have never received one cent in the way of *bounty*, and the statute books do not shew any branch of their business that is even *encouraged*, save the manufacture of coarse cotton goods. Is this fair? Does it become the *protected* to charge the unprotected with aiming at "monopolies," because they ask an application of the very principles to their own pursuits which they have frankly yielded to the pursuits of others? These are words of truth and soberness, and I appeal to every honest man for an answer.

I shall now speak briefly of the cotton manufacture, and esteem myself fortunate if I can refer to the conduct of *some*, without being led away by my feelings, at their *ungrateful* and *ungracious* interference.

The duty on coarse cottons is almost equal to 100 per cent. on the value of such imported articles, of seeming like quality — yet the practical operation of that duty has been to effect a real, solid and substantial deduction in the price of such goods — the domestic being cheaper than the foreign ever were, regard being had to strength and durability. It is estimated that our coarse shirtings will wear three times as long as those which were heretofore received from the East Indies — and yet the nominal price is about the same, or less. Thus every person in the United States concerned in this business, from the cotton planter to his slave who uses the cloth, is benefitted by the "prohibitory duty" on these goods.

This prohibition, like all other prohibitions, came from the people of the eastern states. In 1810, there were only 269 establishments in all the states — of which 108 were located in New Hampshire, Massachusetts, (proper), Rhode Island and Connecticut — the most of the last were large establishments, many of the others small. I cannot speak certainly, but it is my opinion, after considerable examination and reflection, that the 108 mills to the eastward contained twice as many spindles as all the rest,* which were also too much scattered to concentrate public opinion as dependent on individual interests. The duty asked for by the people of the east was opposed by those of the south, but New York and Pennsylvania threw in their weight on the side of the former, and the "prohibition" was thus *secured*. Since then, when the wool and hemp growers, and manufacturers, the iron makers, &c. of these and other states, were striving to obtain encouragement (not *prohibition*), in favor of their own industry, certain of those very cotton manufacturers sent quantities of their goods to Washington, labelled "WE WANT NO

* The returns of the marshals in 1810 do not give the amount of spindles — but the following will shew that our assertion is a safe one:

Massachusetts — value of cotton and wool spun in mills		$931,906
Rhode Island		305,824
		1,237,730
New York — as above	9,225	
Pennsylvania	354,692	
		363,917
Difference		$873,813

FURTHER PROTECTION," to defeat those to whom they had been indebted for the protection which they enjoyed! Generous souls! — they were content with the *prohibition* that they had — we ought to have expected that they would ask a "BOUNTY!" But they were moderate — they were satisfied with *cent per cent*. Here was realized the moral of the fable of the Fox and Goat that had fallen into a well — the former persuaded the latter to rear himself against the side of the well, that he, (the fox), by mounting on his horns, might jump out, when he would pull out the goat; but, no sooner was Reynard relieved of his difficulty, than he gravely advised his late companion in distress to reconcile himself to *starvation,* for it was impossible to suppose that he would run any risk, or put himself to the least trouble to return the act of kindness received — and he laughed at the goat's long beard and sober countenance, wondering that, with so much apparent wisdom, he should have been so silly as to suppose that any one who was doing "very well" should concern himself about others differently conditioned.

It is, however, nothing more than simple justice to say, that this *meanest of acts* was deprecated by the cotton manufacturers generally, as severely as it was by any other persons among us — and I know some of the opponents of the tariff who used this thing to advance their cause, and yet regarded the authors of it just as the British respected *Benedict Arnold* after they had purchased him. — They loved the treason, but despised the traitor.

So much for the *eastern* opposition to the encouragement of domestic industry, unless applied to the things in which they themselves hold, or can obtain a "monopoly" of. But these men are going into disrepute, and the east will give a decided support to the middle and west, though some may still talk of "monopolies" and "prohibitions," to blind the public understanding and divert attention from themselves. The southern opposition grows out of different principles — more liberal and just than those which I have exposed, but built upon the same opinions that originally led them to resist the discrimina-tory duties on tonnage and the establishment of a navy — which, in respect to those things, they have entirely abandoned, in the belief that they are for the common good of the country, as they will yet be convinced that domestic manufactures are, by reason of the *home market* afforded for their productions. . . .

Condy Raguet, editor of The Banner of The Constitution

Ironical petition of oystermen and others, designed to shew the absurdity of laws restricting industry.

PETITION

To the Honourable the Senate and House of Representatives of the United States: *The petition of the subscribers most respectfully represents,* THAT your petitioners are inhabitants of the district of country which borders upon the river Delaware, and have been long engaged in the business of catching rock-fish and perch, in raking oysters, and in shooting wild ducks for the Philadelphia market — that in the pursuit of their respective occupations, your petitioners have set in motion a great quantity of *American industry,* such as that employed in fishing, and shooting, in boat-building, in navigating, and in selling fish and game in the market, and in transporting oysters in carts or wheelbarrows to the numerous oyster cellars of the city — that your petitioners are great admirers of the "American System," inasmuch as it teaches the glorious truth, that home industry ought to be protected against foreign rivalship, and that it is unpatriotic for a people to send abroad for things which can be produced by themselves at home — that,

holding these truths to be self evident, your petitioners have seen, with extreme regret, the completion of the Delaware and Chesapeake canal, which, owing to the superior abundance of fish, oysters, and wild ducks, on the waters of the Chesapeake, enables the fishermen, the oystermen, and the duck shooters, of Maryland, *a foreign State,* to undersell your petitioners in the home market — that this introduction of foreign fish, oysters and wild ducks, creates an unfavourable balance of trade against Philadelphia, by which a large amount of specie will be drained from her, which was not the case when your petitioners had the command of the home market, for they, in exchange for their fish, oysters and wild ducks, were in the habit of taking dry goods, groceries and liquors — that the notion entertained by many people, that it is good policy to buy cheap instead of dear, is one of the fallacies of the Free Trade System, and is very clearly so to your petitioners, who think that it would be manifestly for the benefit of the citizens of Philadelphia to buy their fish, oysters and wild ducks, at double price, rather than encourage the industry of foreigners, for it is humbly conceived that Maryland is as much a foreign state to

Condy Raguet, *The Principles of Free Trade* (Philadelphia: Carey, Lea and Blanch, 1835), pp. 13–14, 49–51. This first appeared in *The Banner of The Constitution* Jan. 13 and Feb. 20, 1830.

27882

Pennsylvania, as Great Britain is to the United States — that, in fine, your petitioners cannot pursue their several vocations without some Congressional aid: —

They therefore pray that your Honourable bodies, by virtue of that power granted by the Constitution, which authorizes any and every act which may be calculated to promote "the general welfare," will impose a tax upon all fish, oysters and wild ducks, which may pass through the canal aforesaid, or entirely prohibit their importation into Philadelphia. And your petitioners, for thus putting money into their pockets, taken out of those of the consumers, will, as in duty bound, ever pray.

Plausibility of the terms "Domestic Industry" and "American System." The consumption of foreign products affords employment to American industry as much as the consumption of domestic products. This proved, by a comparison of the two modes of converting raw cotton into fabrics, the commercial process, and the manufacturing process.

THERE is something so captivating in the term "Domestic Industry," and something so patriotic in the term "American System," that it is not to be wondered at, that the party which first seized upon those expressions as watch words, should have succeeded with the mass of the people, and have carried their point by a *coup de main.* The time once was, when, by "domestic industry" was meant the industry of the farmer, the planter, the miller, the mariner, the merchant, the mechanic, the tradesman, the day labourer, the artizan, and, in fine, all the various individuals, who by their industry contributed to advance the wealth of the nation and the prosperity of the people. At the present day it signifies very little

more than the industry of the very few persons who are employed in the spinning and weaving of cotton and wool, and who do not comprise more than one in every one hundred of the whole population. In vain is it urged upon the champions of the "American System," that foreign commodities can only be procured in exchange for domestic commodities, and that domestic commodities can only be produced by the employment of domestic industry. They will not believe that the industry of Pennsylvania, which is employed in the raising of wheat, pork, butter, lard, beef, whiskey, corn, hams, linseed oil, wagons, carts, carriages, harness, saddlery, hats, boots, shoes, books, stationary, and a hundred other articles, and which are exchanged with the cotton, rice, and tobacco growers of the South, for bills on Great Britain, with which she pays for the manufactures she imports from that country, is domestic industry; for, if they did so believe, they would never repeat, so steadily, the exploded argument, that to import foreign fabrics is to be tributary to foreign industry.

When we reflect upon the tenacity with which this doctrine is adhered to, contrary to the clearest demonstration, for its falsity is as self evident as that two and two are four, we are almost tempted to regard as hopeless all expectations of seeing the public mind enlightened upon this important subject. When we hear men, some of them too the most conspicuous politicians of the country, pronounce with great earnestness their conviction, that to import foreign fabrics is paying foreign tribute — that the American cotton manufacturers enter into successful competition with the British in foreign markets, when they are not able to do it in the home market, without a protection of from 25 to 175 per cent. — that experience shews that the effects of high duties are to reduce the prices of commodities below what they would be without them — that high duties instead of diminishing commerce, increase it — that the way for a nation to grow rich, is to refuse to purchase the products of other nations, and thereby to diminish the extent of the sales of her own products; — when, we say, we hear such doctrines as these, advanced as the doctrines of sound political economy, we are persuaded that, in order to produce a change of opinion, *reason* is not the faculty of the mind which is to be addressed. As well might a teacher of mathematics attempt to instruct in the principles of that science a scholar, who, at the threshold, should refuse to admit that two parallel lines can never meet, or that any two sides of a triangle are greater than the third. The powerful reasoning of Adam Smith, the clear demonstrations of Say, and the forcible and able expositions of McCulloch, would have no more influence in effecting a change of the views of some we could name, than if they were the wild and silly effusions of ignorant declaimers.

IV   MEMORIALS FROM CONVENTIONS

Memorial from the Protectionist Convention held at New York, October 26, 1831

. . . It is a settled axiom, that the industry of a nation is in proportion to the capital devoted to its maintenance. It is, therefore, thought to be a wise policy to multiply the inducements to apply capital to the employment of labour at home, rather than to the purchase abroad and traffic in commodities of foreign production, by which, the capital of the country is made to set in motion foreign labour. This is founded on the principle, universally admitted, that there is, in every nation a power or capability of labour beyond that actually put forth; and that its effective industry is proportioned to the stimulus applied in the shape of capital. This constitutes the American System. It invites the application of American capital to stimulate American industry. It imposes a restriction, in the form of an impost duty, on certain products of *foreign* labour; but so far as relates to *American* capital, or *American* labour, it simply offers security and inducement to the one, and gives energy and vigour to the other. The purpose of the protective system being thus directed to the utmost expansion of the industry of the nation into every channel of domestic competition, it would seem to be manifestly erroneous to call such a system *restrictive*, inasmuch as the avenues of labour in the internal organization of any community are much more numerous and extensive, than those which belong to foreign trade: whilst, on the other hand, there are no restrictions so

Hezekiah Niles, *Journal of The Proceedings of the Friends of Domestic Industry*, New York, Oct. 26, 1831 (Baltimore, 1831), pp. 18–35.

severe upon the occupation of our citizens, and none that so irresistibly impel labour into a small number of channels as those that are created by the capital and industry of older nations when concentrated and brought into competition with the capital and industry of a young people in their first attempts to possess themselves of the arts that create and accumulate wealth. A nation that is devoted to agriculture only, and is dependent upon foreign labour for its manufactures, presents the spectacle of a people whose industry is confined to the single occupation of cultivating the soil, and transporting its products abroad, and is always subject to be disturbed by the policy of those on whom it depends for the purchase of its products: but the same nation, when encouraged in the attempt to supply itself with manufactured fabrics, releases its labour from the restraints of its previous straitened condition, and is seen rapidly diversifying its pursuits until they finally cover the whole space that was originally divided between itself and the people that supplied it with manufactures. . . .

. . . Revulsions in trade are unavoidable: the balance of supply and demand cannot always be regulated with precision. There is a tendency, growing out of a prosperous commerce, to push success to an extreme which produces reaction. To these periods of embarrassment, of general stagnation, and severe pressure for money, the United States have been peculiarly subject. — We attribute this, in a great measure, to our having depended, in so great a degree, for our manufactures, upon the nations of Europe. Importation is induced more frequently by the necessity or hope of the manufacturer to find a market, than by actual reference to the wants or means of the country. A reduction in the prices of exports, following

an excessive importation, causes a state of exchange which leads to an exportation of specie; the moment this exportation touches that portion of the precious metals necessary to sustain the money circulation, the operations of the banks become embarrassed, and distress and dismay are spread through all classes of the community.

We believe that the system which furnishes a nation with manufactures, essential to its daily wants, from its own industry, is the best possible security against violent changes in its currency; — changes which paralize all industry, and disturb all trade; and we therefore submit it to the experience and judgment of the American people whether the protective system is not, in this particular, more advantageous to the country than that which, after deluging our markets with foreign manufactures, draws from us, in return, not a useless commodity, but the instrument by which our exchanges are performed, the very basis of our bank circulation, the essential principle of commercial confidence.

Mistaken opinions in regard to the effect of the tariff upon the prices of commodities used in the United States and upon which the protective system has been brought to bear, have furnished some popular objections against the wisdom of the policy. It has been said that the effect of a duty is necessarily to increase the price of any article upon which it is laid to the full amount of the tax. It would be easy to show, by a minute survey of the whole field of American industry, that, so far from this being true, the invariable operation of the tariff has been to lower the price to the consumer of every article that has been successfully manufactured under the protection. Such a survey would require more detail than the purpose of this address allows, but we propose to examine the operation of the tariff upon some of our most important staples.

In the article of cotton it is admitted that our manufacture has arrived at such perfection in the production of the coarse fabrics, that they are not only furnished at little more than one half of the cost which the imported articles of the same kind bore a few years ago, but they are produced as cheaply at the present time as our foreign rivals, under all the excitements of American competition, are able to furnish them. They have had a constant and increasing demand for several years for exportation as well as for home consumption. None but the finer qualities are now imported, which are little, if at all affected by the minimum duty. The price of raw cotton has fallen but about a cent a pound within the last four years, whilst the price of cotton goods, — of sheetings, for instance, of more than three yards to the pound, — has fallen nearly four cents a yard within the same period. Satinetts, of wool and cotton, are made at less than one half the price of cassimeres, and are more durable. Cotton flannels formerly imported from China at from fifty to sixty cents a yard, are now made, of a better quality, here, at from fifteen to twenty cents. Indeed we might enumerate every species of manufacture in which this material enters as a component part, to show that both in the character of the article and the cheapness of its price, the country has been a great gainer since the enactment of the system that has promoted its fabrication.

To the cotton planters of the United States, the system has undoubtedly yielded the most decisive advantages. It has created a certain and valuable market for about one-fifth of their crop, and it has encouraged the consumption of large quantities of their staple in fabrics to which it never would have been applied, if the manufacture had not been carried on in our own country. The establishment of cotton mills amongst us has had the most visible tendency to induce our manufacturers to apply cotton to uses which both the policy and the position of foreign manufacturers would have forever forbidden them from adopting. This fact is conspicuously seen in the application of cotton to sail cloth, and to all those articles of heavy clothing in which it has lately been substituted for wool. It is now manufactured into carpets, blankets, cordage, twine, net work and a variety of other commodities that may be said to be exclusively of American origin. Cotton being a product of our own soil, we have naturally an interest to extend its application to new uses, above what might be expected from nations who are mere purchasers of the article, and who are as much, if not more, concerned in preserving and promoting the use of wool and hemp in the fabrics to which we have applied our cotton.

Let us next consider the article of Iron; and we will introduce the notice of it with a quotation from that masterly report of the first Secretary of the Treasury, which, forty years ago, recommended prohibitory duties in favor of the manufacturers of this article: "for" says that report, "they are entitled to pre-eminent rank. None are more essential in their kinds, none so extensive in their uses. They constitute, in whole or in part, the implements or the materials, or both, of almost every useful occupation. Their instrumentality is every where conspicuous. It is fortunate for the United States that they have peculiar advantages, for deriving the full benefit, of this most valuable material, and they have every motive to improve it with systematic care. It is to be found in various parts of the United States in great abundance, and of almost every quality; and fuel, the chief instrument in manufacturing it, is both cheap and plenty." This report which is a treatise on Political Economy, at least equal to anything that has appeared since its publication, states that the average price of Iron before the revolution, was about sixty-four dollars per ton, and that at the time of that report it was about eighty dollars. Soon after it appears to have risen to ninety-five dollars, and in 1814 was as high as one hundred and fifty dollars. After the ineffectual Tariff of 1818, which ruined numbers, induced by its vain protection to make investments in the manufacture of iron, it rose from ninety to one hundred and five dollars per ton. Under the influence of the duties of the acts of 1824 and 1828, it has declined to its present prices of from seventy-five to eighty-five dollars per ton, and there is every reason for the confident belief entertained, that if our own market be protected against the formidable and incessant endeavours of the British manufacturers to controul it, the price of iron will, before long, decline to from fifty to sixty dollars per ton. Such is the irrefutable proof of all recent experience. — Cut nails, which in 1816 sold for twelve cents per lb. are now sold for less than half that sum, under the permanent security of five cents per lb. which has given our manufacturers their own market. "The United States, (says Hamilton's report before mentioned) already in great measure supply themselves with nails. About one million eight hundred thousand pounds of nails and spikes were imported into the United States, in the course of the year ending the 4th of September 1790. A duty of two cents per lb, would, it is presumable, speedily put an end to so considerable an importation. And it is in every view proper that an end should be put to it."

Bar Iron which sold at Pittsburgh in 1829 at $122, sells there now at $95. Castings which were $63 are now $50 per ton. Such are the practical results, proving the operation of the tariffs on the market for iron. The duty, by the law of 1816, was so inadequate as to cause nothing but ruin to those concerned and enhancement of price to the consumer. The act of 1818 was some amelioration; the acts of 1824 and 1828, which increased the duty, decreased the price. Hammered bar iron under a duty of twenty-two dollars and forty cents a ton; is at a lower price than when under a duty of nine dollars a ton, and improved in quality from five to ten per cent by the greater care and skill which more extensive investment has naturally created under more certain protection. — The efforts of the English manufacturers to destroy the American manufacture of iron, and possess themselves of our market, have occasioned extensive bankruptcies amongst them in England, and reduced the price of iron considerably below the cost of manufacture; insomuch that a convention of iron manufacturers, recently held there, resolved to reduce the quantity made twenty per cent throughout the United Kingdoms. With the controul of our market they would infallibly regulate both the price and the quantity of the iron in this country — thirty-one establishments of which have appeared in Western Pennsylvania alone, since the last Tariff act.

The influence of protection upon wool, while it has been most beneficial upon the farming states, has had no tendency, that we are aware of, to injure the plantation states. The number of sheep in the United States is computed at about twenty millions: And their increase at about five millions since the act of 1828, which gave a great impulse to the stock. The farmers of Virginia, Pennsylvania,

Ohio, New-York and the other wool-growing states, have an interest in this national property, taken at fifty-five cents per lb., nearly equal to the capital of the plantation states in the cotton crop of this year, reckoning it at thirty millions of dollars. There is no doubt that, within three years to come, the farming capital in wool will be more valuable than the plantation capital in cotton. Without protecting duties American wool would be reduced one-half in quantity and in price. The large flocks which now cover the immense and inexhaustible pastures of the United States, most of them more or less of the fine Spanish breeds, must be again slaughtered, as has been heretofore the case, for want of due protection, and this great capital in fleece sacrificed to that of cotton with enormous loss to one interest, and with no possible advantage to the other. For like every thing else, woollen goods have fallen from twenty to twenty-five per cent since the last tariff. The immediate effect of that act, by calling a large number of additional clothiers into active enterprise, was to cause a decline in prices ruinous to many of those before engaged in the occupation. Under the influence of the improvement in the price of wool, woollen manufacturers have rallied again, but, at least as respects them, the charge of monopolizing prices is a cruel mockery. The advantages of the Tariff, in its operation upon wool, have thus far been confined almost exclusively to the farming interest; the manufacturers have yet all their way to win, and the effect of that competition, which is the result of protection, cannot be known until it has had longer time for operation.

The finest cotton and woollen manufactures are not yet much made in the United States, but we may assert without fear of contradiction that nine-tenths of the American people, who do not affect for-

eign luxuries and fashions, may be clothed with woollen, cotton, fur and leather fabrics of their own country, better and cheaper, than either could have been obtained abroad if the tariff had never been enacted. The greatest mistakes prevail in this respect; it is continually said, that hats, coats, boots and other articles of dress are dearer here than elsewhere. Such is not the case with all those who are independent of foreign fashions. Those who enjoy superior wealth and study superior elegance, are at liberty to gratify their caprice, at that additional expense, which such a gratification costs in all countries — in none more than in Great Britain, where the opulent and noble are in the habit of paying more extravagantly for French, Asiatic and other luxuries, than some of our opulent citizens chuse to pay, in like manner, for luxuries imported from abroad.

Whilst we assert that it has been the effect of the protective system to benefit the consumers by giving them manufactures cheaper than they had them before, we are willing to admit that prices have had a correspondent fall in the same articles abroad; but this fall of price abroad has been the result of the competition of American labour. It is impossible to advert to the fact that the United States export to foreign markets six times the quantity of domestic manufactures that they exported in 1820, and at present furnish incomparably the largest share of the home demand, without perceiving the tendency of such a competition to reduce the price of the same articles amongst all those nations who aim at supplying us.

But we hold it to be a common error to consider the comparative cheapness of the foreign and domestic commodity a test of the value of the system. Even if it were true that the domestic product were not reduced in price, and were to be procured only at a higher cost than the foreign, still the benefit of the system would be found in the fact that it enables the domestic consumer to afford the higher price for the manufacture, and thereby to furnish himself on better terms than he could have done when obliged to depend upon the foreign imported commodity — that, in other words, the increase of price, if it has taken place, cannot be called a tax upon the consumer, if the same system which has increased the price has also increased his means of paying it. That this increased ability to pay has occurred to a most beneficial extent, is evident in the invigorated condition of our agriculture in the last three or four years, during which period the value of the labour of the farmer, and with it the value of his land, it is well known, has risen some twenty or thirty per cent. This augmentation in the value of agricultural labour and capital can be ascribed to no other cause than to the increase of the manufacturing classes, and to the rapid growth of our home market under the protective system. During this period there have been no wars to create a demand abroad for our grain, but on the contrary, all the producing nations have been exerting their industry to the utmost, and maintaining a rivalry against our own citizens which would have visited them with the most disastrous consequences if they had not found a steady and valuable market at home. The fact, too, that agricultural products have risen whilst manufactured goods have fallen, furnish the best proofs that the fall of prices are to be mainly attributable to the competition of domestic labour.

The loudest complaints of oppression proceed from the South, particularly from South Carolina; but that these complaints are not owing to the tariff acts, is unquestionably proved by the fact, that their public press, their memorials to Congress, and other mediums of complaint, were as much burthened with them before those acts, as they have been since. In the acquisition of the extensive and fertile territories annexed to the United States by the purchase of Louisiana the lands and property of the plantation states could not fail to be depreciated, by a vast accession of lands, at least as fertile, for all similar purposes. But it is inconceivable how a steady market for at least two hundred thousand bales of cotton a year, liable to no fluctuation from foreign influence, can be injurious to the cotton-growing states; and, certainly, if the inhabitants of the less exuberant and more industrious latitudes of the central and eastern states, were not, from the influence of climate, or some other cause, less liable to excitement and less addicted to complain than their southern brethren, they have had much greater cause for it.

The breadstuffs, lumber, and nearly all the other staples of all the grain growing states are excluded from European markets by prohibitory duties. Whilst the export of cotton has quadrupled, that of breadstuffs has diminished in a much greater ratio with relation to the population of the states that produce them. If instead of spending their time in unavailing complaints, they had not conformed to circumstances, and turned their attention to manufactures, *their* grievances would have been infinitely greater than any of which the southern states have ever complained. Nothing could relieve the farming interests of the middle states but their own manufactures and the manufactures of the eastern states. They alone supply that market which Europe denies. In addition to the incalculable consumption of breadstuffs by the manufacturers of the grain-growing states, what is equivalent to a million of barrels of their breadstuffs is imported every year into the eastern states; a relief, without which, the susceptibility of these states would have been tried to a degree of endurance far beyond that exacted from their brethren of the south. It cannot escape observation, that while their sufferings are announced in most eloquent language, and in unintermitting remonstrance, yet there has been so little specification of the supposed causes, that it is denied by many, among themselves that they suffer at all. There is even good reason to believe that within the last five years, the interest on planting capital has been more productive to the owner, than the interest on the same amount of capital employed in manufactures. . . .

The policy of the protective system is happily and amply illustrated in the growth and prosperity of the United States. The union teems with proofs of its wisdom. All that Hamilton's masterly report predicted of its benefits, has been unfolded and is progressive beyond the most sanguine anticipation. All the objections refuted in his argument have disappeared in experience. The antagonists of the system not long since declared that it would infallibly diminish, if not destroy the revenue, and compel a resort to loans and taxes for the support of government: their present complaint is that the revenue is excessive. Redundant importations, some years ago, imposed the necessity of a loan; the manufacturing establishments now spreading throughout the United States, sustain their agriculture, have revived their commerce, have vastly increased their coasting trade and domestic exchanges, and have mainly contributed to an abundance of the precious metals; they are the stablest pledges of independence and permanent peace, and the most accessible objects of taxation and productive resources in case of need. . . .

Memorial from the Free Trade Convention held at Philadelphia, September and October, 1831

It is self-evident that the industry of a country is most profitably employed, or, in other words, that a country acquires the greatest wealth, and its general prosperity is most advanced, in proportion as its capital and labor are most productive.

It is not less obvious that, if a given amount of capital and labor produces in the same time a less quantity of a certain commodity than could have been purchased with that quantity of another article which might have been produced in the same time by the same amount of capital and labor, there has been a misapplication of such capital and labor, and a national loss equal to the difference between the quantity produced and that which might have been purchased with the proceeds of the same capital and labor otherwise applied. . . .

A state of society may indeed exist, where, owing either to a superabundant

Albert Gallatin, "Memorial of the Committee of the Free Trade Convention, September and October, 1831," in F. W. Taussig, ed., *State Papers and Speeches on the Tariff* (Cambridge: Harvard University, 1893), pp. 119–212.

population, to over taxation, to a great inequality in the distribution of wealth or in the means of acquiring it, or to any other natural or artificial cause, a portion of an industrious population may occasionally or at all times be in actual want of employment. Of a country thus situated, it may be said that it contains a capability of labor beyond that actually put forth. The symptoms of such a state of things are sufficiently visible; workmen discharged or with reduced wages, asking employment and food, and poor rates given to able-bodied men as a supplement to their insufficient salary. We may understand how in that case a new manufacture — some new channels opened to the national industry — would, by giving employment to the laborer, bring into action an additional amount of labor.

There may also be countries favored with a more genial climate, where the wants being few, and the absolute necessary means of subsistence earned with less labor, long continued misgovernment has created deeply rooted habits of indolence. And such countries may also be said to have a dormant power of labor which a free and wise government might stimulate and put in motion.

The situation of the United States is the very reverse in both respects. The existing rates of wages stimulate industry with a greater force than in any other country; and, as a natural consequence, there is not on the face of the globe a nation encumbered with less indolence or idleness; a population more active, industrious, and, we believe, more productive. This will continue "so long as the cheapness of unimproved land shall offer a certain employment to labor, and so long as the constitution remains free as it is." If the restrictionists can find a more powerful cause, some more efficient means to stimulate labor, and render American industry more productive and profitable, it will be a great and glorious discovery. For if it may perhaps be admitted that the national progress in acquiring wealth may be tested by the general rate of profits, there can be no doubt, and the most conspicuous illustration of the fact is found in the situation of the United States compared with that of every other country that the greatest mass of comfort and happiness is always found where the renumeration of labor is the highest. Should this prove to be one of the obstacles to the establishment of some manufactures, we nevertheless pray that it may long so continue. . . .

. . . it is principally respecting the increased consumption, by the protected manufactures, of supplies of domestic origin other than the raw materials, and, above all, of breadstuffs and other provisions, that the most exaggerated accounts have been industriously circulated. It might be supposed, from the language held on that subject, that the agricultural interest was exclusively indebted for its prosperity to the restrictive system. We are told of the "invigorated condition of our agriculture in the last three or four years, during which period the value of the labor of the farmer, and with it the value of his land, it is well known, has risen some 20% or 30%," and that "this augmentation in the value of agricultural labor and capital can be ascribed to no other cause than to the increase of the manufacturing classes, and to the rapid growth of our home market under the protecting system."

On hearing this, and also that what was equivalent to one million of barrels of breadstuffs was imported every year into the eastern States, we sought for proofs, and find the average price of flour at

Philadelphia to have been for the eleven years, 1820 to 1830, —

1820,	$4.72	1825,	$5.10
1821,	4.78	1826,	4.65
		1827,	5.23
Average	4.75		4.99
1822,	$6.58	1828,	$5.60
1823,	6.82	1829,	6.35
1824,	5.62	1830,	4.98
Average	6.34		5.64

Average for the eleven years, $5.49. If it is due to the protecting system that the average of the last three years, as compared with the three immediately preceding, rose from 5% to 5.64%, to what cause must be ascribed the still higher average of 6.34% for the years 1822 to 1824, immediately following the depressed price of 4.75% of the years 1820 to 1821, and before the country was under the magic influence of the tariffs of 1824 and 1828? Was the depression to the average price of $5, during the years 1825 to 1827, the result of the tariff of 1824, or that to the same price, in 1830, of the tariff of 1828?

The enlightened advocates of the protecting system need not be informed that all those fluctuations are exclusively due to the foreign demand; that in a country which always raises what is the equivalent of fifteen hundred thousand barrels of breadstuffs beyond its own consumption, the price depends on the proportion between that supply and the foreign demand; and that that demand will continue to govern the price of the home market, whatever may be the increase of the domestic consumption, so long as such an excess beyond that consumption shall continue to be raised. If there was no foreign demand for that surplus (or for any other article which is now extensively exported), either the quantity raised must

be diminished in that proportion, or the price would fall to the very lowest rate at which the produce can be cultivated. Such has been the invariable result in every part of the country too distant from the seaports to participate in the benefit of the foreign market. The enhanced price of breadstuffs and other exportable articles, beyond that minimum, is almost exclusively due to the foreign demand, and not in any perceptible degree to the increase of manufactures. The statement of prices exhibits no other than those ordinary fluctuations in the foreign demand which have at all times occurred, and does not afford the slightest proof of that permanent improvement in the value of agricultural labor ascribed to the protecting system. For the enhanced price which the farmer obtains for any of his products which continue to be extensively exported, he continues to be solely indebted to the foreign market and to commerce. . . .

It is, therefore, only when the supply of the domestic manufacture is, or may within a very short time be made, equal to the full demand of the country, that domestic competition may reduce the rate of profits, and ultimately the cost of production. It cannot be doubted that, when the competition is with foreign articles, the necessity of introducing the improvements requisite for that purpose is much greater than when it is only between the American manufacturers. When the manufacture is already established at the time of laying the protecting duty, the improvements which may afterwards take place would have been introduced at least as early, if the restrictive system had not existed; and there may be instances where the duty prevents or retards the adoption of such improvements.

But a reduction of price is, in no case whatever, due to the tariff, so long as the similar foreign article can still be imported, and the price of the domestic commodity is not reduced below that at which the foreign is sold. Under those circumstances, the reduction is clearly due to a fall in the price of the foreign article, and is altogether independent of the tariff. If, in any instance, the price of the domestic article has, immediately after the tariff, fallen below the price at which the foreign article could, thenceforth, be imported, it only proves that the duty was higher than was necessary for the ostensible object in view. The price must fall as low as that at which the foreign article might have been purchased prior to the protecting duty, before the national loss caused by it ceases. It is only then that the domestic manufacture proves successful and beneficial to the consumer, and to the community at large.

Coarse cotton goods are the only protected branch which comes within that description, and the causes of the fall of price, which operated almost simultaneously in England and America, are notorious and acknowledged. They cannot be better expressed than in the words of one of the manufacturers (Mr. Dexter) examined before the Committee on Manufactures in 1828. "It is owing to the improvement in machinery, the reduced price of raw cotton, and the increased skill in the manufacture." The reduction in the price of the raw material was solely due to the increased supply compared with the demand. The manufacture was already firmly established before the year 1816. As early as the year 1810, there were north of the Potomac fifty mills for spinning cotton in operation, and twenty-five more that went into operation the ensuing year. The weaving business had commenced, but was not so far advanced. Under those circumstances, the improvements in machinery and the gradual acquisition of skill would have infallibly

taken place with the common average duty, which was, at that time, about 33% on the value. It is at least doubtful whether the favorable result was hastened by the tariff of 1816, which gave a protecting duty of six cents and a quarter per yard, amounting to 62½% actual, and equivalent to 52% nominal duty ad valorem on the prime cost of the cheapest India cotton goods at that time imported.

A similar fall of price, and owing to the same causes, took place in England notwithstanding the partial competition of East India goods. . . .

We will only observe here, that the decline of price in the Pittsburgh iron, which cannot be ascribed to that of the foreign article, is also independent of the tariff. The iron works of west Pennsylvania were, and still continue to be, protected against foreign iron; and that made within one hundred miles of the seashore, by the expense of transportation, which is still $40, and prior to the last war amounted to $80 a ton. Considerable fortunes were made by the owners of the establishments which were directed with skill, frugality, and a sufficient capital; but there being no competition, the iron was dear, and of inferior quality. The price of transportation was greatly diminished some time after the peace, and the Juniata iron, of a superior quality, was brought to Pittsburgh, at the expense of $30, and sold for $100 to $120 a ton. This, united with unfavorable circumstances under which the western country then labored, prostrated the iron works for a while. But there was no intrinsic impediment; and with more experience, by the partial application of coal and various other improvements, the iron business has been revived, and the price of iron, of much better quality than formerly, reduced to about ninety dollars. The competition of the Juniata iron operated, in this instance, in the same manner as if it had been of foreign origin. Had it not been for it, the iron of west Pennsylvania would neither have been improved in quality, or have declined in price. And this effect has been produced without the slightest assistance from the tariff, or any other cause, with the same competition to encounter, and through no other means but a judicious application of skill and enterprise.

The only effect that can possibly be ascribed to a protecting duty is that of encouraging the establishment of manufactures which would not otherwise have existed, or of inducing a greater number of persons to embark in those already existing. The propriety of the duty depends altogether on the probability of speedy success, that is to say, of the manufacture being so far adapted to the circumstances of the country that, after having been assisted by the duty in surmounting the first difficulties incident to every new undertaking, it will be able to sustain itself, and without such assistance to compete with the foreign article. It has been clearly shown that the manufacture is otherwise a losing concern, productive of national loss. . . .

The manufacture of cast and bar iron was one of the few which had been established in America, under the colonial Government. It owed its origin to the destruction of the English forests, and the abundance of wood in America. The price of bar iron is stated to have been at that time $64 a ton and to have risen to about $80 in the year 1790. The application of bituminous coal, and other improvements in the manufacture, have produced a revolution, which has increased the annual quantity of malleable iron made in England from seventy to more than six hundred thousand tons, and has enabled her to sell the various descriptions of the species called "rolled iron" at a lower price than that at which any species whatever can be afforded anywhere else. Notwithstanding the acknowledged superiority of that of Russia and Sweden for certain purposes, the cheapness of the British manufacture has lessened the demand for that of every other country, and seems ultimately to have affected the price of every species. Although it had not, in 1816, been yet reduced to its present rate, Congress was induced to raise, by the tariff of that year, the duty on rolled iron from 15% ad valorem, to a specific duty of $30 a ton, equivalent at that time to about 67% on the value. This was again, in 1828, raised to $37 a ton, which on account of the progressive fall in the price of that article, is now equivalent, according to the official statement of imposts for 1830, to an average duty of 113½% on the value of the whole amount of the different qualities of that species which are imported into the United States. The specific duty of $9 a ton, laid in 1816, on hammered or Swedish and Russian iron, did not exceed the former rate of 15% ad valorem. It was raised in 1818 to $15, in 1824 to $18, and in 1828 to $22.40, which is equivalent to a duty of 40% ad valorem.

It appears that, notwithstanding those high duties, the importations either of bar iron, or of the total amount of the manufactures of which it is the principal material, instead of being lessened, have gradually increased. . . .

We need not dwell on the injustice and mischievous effects of an exaggerated duty on an article of such general use as iron. It falls upon the farmer, the mechanic, the shipping interest, and on every branch of the iron manufacture, those few excepted which have been embraced by the partial protecting system; and it operates, in the most unequal and unjust manner, on those parts of the country which have no iron of their own, and might be supplied on cheaper terms under a rational system of moderate duties. The only reason why the extravagant duty is not universally opposed is because the tax thus laid on the agriculturist and the mechanic is spread, over such an extent of country, and falls upon so many, that the amount paid by each, levied as it is indirectly and in small portions at a time, is not generally understood. Those who do understand and feel it have not individually a sufficient interest in the result to induce a general and efficient combination. The law has created a monopoly in favor of the owners of beds of ore, who, unable to supply the wants of the country, will not permit it to be supplied from other quarters. They may easily combine, and their interest, when compared with that of the mechanics and scattered agriculturists, has, here as elsewhere, been found too powerful. This is so true that when an equally or more powerful interest was opposed to theirs they were obliged to yield, and the importation of iron intended for railroads was permitted under the moderate duty of 15%. We approve this measure as being founded on the best interests of the country. We only ask that the same principle be applied to the community at large. There is no other difference between this case and that of agriculture, or any other important branch of industry, than that, in one case, the amount of the tax, presented as a whole, made its pernicious effects at once visible, whilst divided, in the other, amongst 50,000 individuals, the aggregate, though equal in amount, does not attract notice. . . .

Your memorialists believe that the ultimate reduction of the price of American to that of the British rolled iron can duly, and ultimately will be accomplished in that western region, which abounds with ore, and in which is found the most extensive formation of bituminous coal that has yet been discovered in any part of the globe; and this also lying so near the surface of the earth, as to render the extraction of the mineral less expensive than anywhere else. But a considerable period of time must elapse before the wants of a population that increases with such unparalleled rapidity can be fully supplied; and, in the mean while, the western country is not, in any degree, affected by the duties on that article. . . .

The restrictive system lessens the amount of the foreign products which would otherwise be imported.

It has, therefore, an immediate tendency to lessen the ever corresponding amount of exports. The avowed declaration of those who are benefited by it, and their general proscription of the trade with foreign nations, announce that such is their object. Retaliations, however unwise, may be provoked by a hostile course of legislation. It cannot be doubted that a great diminution of the exportations will be the necessary consequence of persevering in that system, to the manifest and great injury of those States which export most, and have no other resources than those exports.

The inhabited part of the United States embraces a territory more extensive and differing more in climate than the whole of western Europe. A necessary and great difference must arise between the branches of industry to which the several portions of that territory are respectively best adapted. This difference is still more increased by that in the nature of the population. The southern States have always confined themselves almost exclusively to the cultivation of the rich products of their climate. This is the only advantage they enjoy, and they owe it to nature. As they make but few, they con-

sume a much greater proportion of manufactured articles imported from other
States or other countries. That system,
therefore, that enhances beyond measure
the price of those objects of necessary
consumption operates most unequally and
unjustly upon them. They are forbidden
to supply themselves on the cheapest
terms consistent with the revenue necessary for the exigencies of Government.
As the greatest consumers they must not
only pay a greater share of the duties
requisite to defray the necessary national
expenditure, but they are compelled to
pay the enhanced price occasioned by the
protecting system. That system cannot be
extended to them. They find in it no in-
demnity, no compensation for the injury
which it inflicts upon them. They have
not, they cannot in self-defense erect manufacturing establishments. The nature of
their population forbids it. Whether from
color or situation is immaterial; the great
mass of the working population of the
southern States is inferior in activity, skill,
and intelligence to that of the other sections of the Union. Where such important
and indelible differences do exist, each
part should be permitted to enjoy its natural advantages; and that legislation is
unjust, unequal, and oppressive which
attempts to confer doubtful benefits on
the one at the expense of the other.

It is idle to say that the southern States
find a compensation in the general advantages in the increased wealth resulting to
the Union from the protecting system.
The fallacy of those pretended advantages has been sufficiently exposed. But,
admitting their reality, they are, according to the doctrines even of the restrictionists, derived from the losses sustained
by the consumers of the South. The duties
on the iron, the woollen manufactures,
the sugar, the salt, and all the other privi-
leged articles which they consume, give
no additional activity or employment to
their labor. The amount of their products
remains the same, and their value may be
lessened; they pay more and receive nothing. In order that they might be placed
on an equal footing with their fellow-
citizens, in order to enable them to erect
manufactures, they stand in more need of
a tariff against those of the eastern States
than the eastern States against those of
England. From that weapon of self-
defense they deprived themselves in
adopting the Constitution of the United
States. . . .

Your memorialists trust that the temporary and doubtful advantages ascribed to
the tariff system, and which may, perhaps, accrue to some particular districts,
will not be permitted to outweigh considerations of a far more important character. It may justly be expected, from the
patriotism of those who calculate upon
such local advantages, that they will not
insist on what is manifestly unjust, and
persevere in a course which disturbs the
peace of the country and alienates the
affections of a numerous portion of their
fellow-citizens. . . .

V CONTEMPORARY ECONOMIC WRITERS

Daniel Raymond: PROTECTING DUTIES

IT may be admitted, that if individuals, or a nation, can buy an article cheaper than they can make it, they had better buy than to make, as a general rule; but to this general rule there are many exceptions, and these exceptions will embrace the policy of protecting duties to as great an extent, as have ever been contended for by the partisans of a restricted trade.

The doctrine, however, of buying, when we can buy cheaper than we can make, as illustrated, or rather, as stated without illustration, by Dr. Smith, is most erroneous and unsound, when applied to individuals. Had he explained what he means by buying cheaper than we can make, the doctrine might, perhaps, have been admitted as correct. But, in the broad terms in which the doctrine is laid down, it is never adopted by prudent individuals, and much less by nations. If an individual were to go upon the principle of buying what it will cost him more to make than to buy, in the ordinary acceptation of the phrase, it would lead him to inevitable ruin. Every case of this kind, depends on its own circumstances.

It may, as an ordinary rule, be better for the tailor to buy his shoes of the shoemaker, than to make them himself, but it may be better to make than to buy them. If he can have constant employment in his own trade, he had better buy his shoes than to make them. If he has not, it may be better to make than to buy them. If a tailor cannot sell his own work, he had better spend a week in making a pair of shoes, than to buy them with the price of an ordinary day's work. Whether it be better for a farmer to buy his own cloaths, and shoes, than to make them, depends entirely on circumstances. Sometimes it is better to do the one, and sometimes the other. If he can buy them with some of the produce of his own industry, "employed in a way in which he has some advantage," better to buy than to make them; if not, he had better make than buy them. A tailor, who can find employment in his trade only one half of his time, had better employ the other half in making shoes and raising corn, than to be idle that time, and buy his shoes and corn at any price, no matter how cheap. So, the farmer, who can only find a market for one half the product of his labour, will find it more for his interests to employ one half of his time in manufacturing various articles, than to buy those articles at any price whatever. If the tailor and shoemaker will take corn for their work, it will probably be better to buy than to make. This, however, will depend on the quantity they will give in exchange. This is a universal principle – a principle upon which all prudent men act. It applies to all classes of people, to communities, as well as to individuals. This is the true meaning of the doctrine of buying, when you can buy cheaper than you can make. But, from the general unqualified manner, however, in which Dr. Smith lays down the doctrine, one would be led to suppose, that in his opinion at least, it would always be better for the tailor to buy his shoes and his corn, than to make

Daniel Raymond, *Thoughts on Political Economy* (Baltimore: Fielding Lucas, Jr., 1820), pp. 360–380.

the one, and raise the other, by his own labour; and that the farmer could never be profitably employed in making cloaths and shoes.

This doctrine, when rightly explained, is as applicable to nations, as to individuals, as indeed, are all other principles of nature. Nature has not made one set of principles for individuals, and another set for nations, which are in opposition to each other. Indeed, nations are not the creatures of nature. Nature made individuals, and established certain laws for their government, out of these man has formed nations.

The principles which are applicable to individuals, are also applicable to nations; but in order to apply them properly, we must consider nations as individuals, distinct in all their parts, and not as part *individual* only. The nation must be considered as one and indivisible. Let this be done, and we shall not be embarrassed with individual interests and rights, as contradistinguished from national rights and interests. Individual interests are perpetually at variance with national interests. Hence the absurdity of supposing, that which is beneficial to individuals is also beneficial to the nation. An individual, or a class of the community, may be benefitted by being permitted to import goods, free of duty, but it does not necessarily follow, that the nation would be benefitted by it.

It may be beneficial to cotton and tobacco-planters, to be permitted to import cotton and woollen cloths for their own consumption, free of duty, from England, because in England they find a market for their produce. They can exchange "some part of the produce of their own industry, employed in a way in which they have some advantage." As regards the cotton and tobacco-planters, distinct from the nation, they are in the situation of the

tailor and shoemaker, who have constant employment in their trades, when it is better for them to buy of each other, the respective products of their labour, than to make for themselves; but taking the whole United States together, as an individual, with a unity of rights and interests, and it may be better for it, to make its own cotton and woollen cloths, than to import them, even at any price; precisely for the same reason, that it is better for the tailor to make his own shoes, when he has nothing else to do, or to employ his unoccupied time in making shoes, than to remain idle, and buy them at any price.

The question in the one case is, has the tailor full employment in his trade, and the answer to this question will determine whether he had better seize hold of the awl and the plough. So, in the case of the nation, the question is, has it full employment in raising tobacco and cotton, and in its other ordinary occupations? if it has not, it will be wiser, and more conducive to its wealth, to employ its unoccupied time in manufacturing cotton and woollen cloths, than to import them from England at any price.

As to the soundness of this principle there can be no doubt. In its application it is universal both to individuals and nations. It is far less variable than the mariner's compass. The only difficulty consists in its application. — In knowing exactly what portion of a nation's time is unoccupied — how much *surplus labour* it has on hand, which might be profitably employed. The perplexity is also increased by the opposition of individual and national interests, and the difficulty of separating them. But the duty of a legislator, when these interests are once distinguished and separated, does not admit of discussion. It may with as much propriety be contended, that one class of citizens should be permitted to smuggle goods, because it is for their benefit, as that another should be permitted to import them at a low tariff, because it is for their benefit, when opposed to the general interests of the nation.

The sophistry of Dr. Smith's reasoning consists in a great measure, in his not discriminating between national and individual interests. He considers the interests of some particular class of citizens, as identical with the interests of the nation, when in reality they are, perhaps, directly opposed. This is the only principle upon which it can be maintained, that, "to give the monopoly of the home market to the product of domestic industry, in any particular art or manufacture, must generally be hurtful."

A measure of government may interfere with the private interests of an individual, or a class of individuals; but if at the same time, it promotes in a greater degree, the interests of a larger class of individuals, it will be beneficial to the nation, and will promote national wealth.

Such are some of the absurd consequences of confoundnig national with individual wealth. Dr. Smith's reasoning would be sound, if it was true, that national and individual interests were never opposed. Common sense, however, teaches us, that they are often opposed.

The question, whether the importation of manufactures should be prohibited, or the tariff raised, does not at all depend upon the fact, that they can be procured by the consumer cheaper in foreign countries, than in his own. Buying goods where they may be had cheapest, may be the best policy for individuals, while buying them where they come dearest, may be the best policy for the nation. Dr. Smith's doctrine cannot be admitted, till he proves, that individual interests are never at variance with national interests.

If it be admitted, that a man had better employ a week in making a pair of shoes, when he has nothing else to do, than to pay the ordinary price of a day's labour for a pair, I should like to know, why the same principle will not apply to a nation. The cases are parallel, if it be admitted, that a nation is a UNITY. If it be not a unity, I should like to know, what it is. — If a plurality, I should like to know whose interest among its members is paramount, or whether each member is to be permitted to pursue his own interest regardless of the public good, and if so whether this would not utterly destroy the social compact.

If a nation has not full employment in its ordinary vocations, is it not better to employ its unoccupied time in manufacturing cotton and woollen cloths, than in doing nothing? And will this not be a saving of just so much, as the cloths would have cost in foreign countries? Suppose a nation has so much unemployed time, as is necessary to manufacture such a quantity of goods, as would cost a million of dollars to purchase in the place where they could be had the cheapest. Suppose, this quantity of goods to be manufactured in consequence of prohibiting the importation of foreign goods, without withdrawing labour from other branches of industry. Now it matters not, at what price these goods come to the consumers, whether double, triple, or quadruple the price, at which they could have been procured at some other place, the saving to the nation will be, a million of dollars, just as certainly as the tailor would save the price of a pair of shoes, by making them when he had nothing else to do. . . .

To show the positive benefit which restrictions and prohibitions on importations of foreign manufactures, may have, in promoting national wealth, let us suppose the unemployed time of the nation, to equal the perpetual idleness of a hundred thousand men. In order to give the nation full employment, and to promote national wealth to the greatest possible degree, we will also suppose, that a hundred thousand men engage in manufactures. That labour they were in the habit of performing, in other occupations, and which afforded them a scanty support, they leave to be performed by the rest of the nation, which of course by giving them full employment, enables them to enjoy in greater abundance, the necessaries and comforts of life. In order to ascertain whether these men can live by their new employment, without any encouragement and protection from the government, by restrictions and prohibitions on importations of those articles, they are employed in manufacturing, several important inquiries must be made.

What quantity of goods can these men manufacture in one year? What is the value of the same quantity of goods of foreign manufacture? What portion of this value did the raw material constitute? What quantity of manual labour did it require to manufacture these goods in the foreign country? In short, what is the comparative expense of manufacturing an equal quantity of goods in the two countries? The result of this inquiry will show whether these men can live by their labour, without encouragement and protection by the government, and what degree of protection is necessary to enable them to carry it on.

The quantity of goods which these hundred thousand men manufacture annually, must sell for enough to pay for the raw materials — for the necessaries and comforts of life consumed by them and their families, while employed in manufacturing the goods: and as they are as meritorious a class of labourers, as any other in the nation, and equally entitled to the favour of the nation, they should be allowed an ordinary share of the necessaries and comforts of life, — a share equal to that enjoyed by other labourers. In addition to this the goods must sell for enough to pay an ordinary profit on the money vested by the capitalists in these manufactories. Unless this is done, the business cannot be prosecuted. Unless the goods sell for enough to pay for the raw material, and the necessaries and comforts of life, consumed by the labourers, while employed in their work, there will be a positive loss to the manufacturers. If a man employed in making shoes cannot sell his work, for as much corn as he eats while at work, he must necessarily starve by his work.

If then the unemployed time of the nation equals the perpetual idleness of a hundred thousand men, and a law which prohibits the importation of foreign manufactures, has the effect of giving employment to a hundred thousand men in manufactures, without at the same time diminishing the amount of agricultural and mercantile industry, the consequence of such a law, will be, to augment national wealth, to the precise amount that the goods would have cost, had they been imported from foreign countries. This effect is produced without diminishing one whit the consumption of the country; but, on the contrary, encouraging it — without depriving the nation of any of the necessaries or comforts of life, but furnishing them in greater abundance. Some classes of society, may perhaps, get less, but others get more. The capacity of the nation, to acquire the necessaries and comforts of life, will be increased to the amount of what has been thus saved; or rather, in proportion to the increase of industry, which is equal to the labour of a hundred thousand men. . . .

But let us apply this doctrine of buying cheap, to manufactures. Before a man can manufacture a piece of cloth, it may be necessary for him to spend five years in learning the trade. It may be necessary to expend a good deal of money in erecting mills and machinery, and the very first piece of cloth he manufactures, may cost him a thousand dollars a yard. — Better, therefore, says Dr. Smith, to buy than to make it. But the doctrine, it will be said, is not to be limited to the first piece of cloth. Let it be extended then, to one year, and then, perhaps, each yard of cloth will cost a hundred dollars; still, therefore, better to buy than to make. But let it be extended to ten or twenty years, and perhaps each yard of cloth may not cost three dollars; and when this comes to be the case, it may be much cheaper, and therefore, better to make than to buy.

The doctrine, therefore, of not making for yourself, what you can buy cheaper than you can make, in the unqualified manner in which Dr. Smith lays it down, is a most absurd and unprovident doctrine, and leads to utter ruin, even in private life, and much more to national ruin. It is a miserable, short-sighted, beggarly policy, calculated to prevent all improvement in the capacity of either individuals or nations, for acquiring the necessaries and comforts of life.

National wealth, is the effect of national industry. If you would increase the effect, you must add new force and power to the cause. A most effectual method to do this, is to give to national industry a monopoly of the home market.

To suppose, as many writers do, that a monopoly of the home market, has a tendency to benefit the rich, instead of the poor, is most absurd. A monopoly of the home market, for corn, may raise the price of corn to the consumer, it is true, but the effect is more than counterbalanced to the labourer, by the greater demand it creates for labour. Many writers have made the price of commodities, and the price of labour, matters of great importance in political economy; but their absolute, or rather nominal price, is of no importance whatever; — it is only their relative price that can affect the labourer. If a labourer is obliged to give five dollars a bushel for corn, and can, at the same time, get five dollars a day for his work, it is just as well for him, as though he could buy corn for fifty cents a bushel, provided he can, at the same time, get only fifty cents a day for labour. The money price of labour, is a matter of no consequence in any country, neither is the money price of the necessaries of life. The proportion which the price of labour bears to the price of the necessaries of life, is the only important thing, as it regards wages, and a monopoly of the home market, must invariably have a tendency to vary this proportion in favour of labour.

Another important advantage, arising from a monopoly of the home market, is the certainty and stability of the demand for the product of industry. All fluctuations in the demand for either the necessaries or comforts of life, produce want and distress among the labourers, who supply the demand. This nation is at present groaning under the distress, caused by a fluctuation in the demand for the product of labour. The national distress in England, arises from the same cause. The consumption does not equal the production, which, as has already been shown, necessarily produces distress. This is always liable to be the case, when the consumption depends on a foreign market. This market is liable to be interrupted by foreign nations. But this is not the case with a domestic market. In this, the demand is always steady, and usually increasing. It is not liable to be interrupted by foreign nations, so long as a nation maintains its independence.

If the whole product of English industry, was clean consumed annually, by the English nation, there would be little or no distress there — there would be no fluctuations in the demand for labour. The product of their industry is abundantly sufficient for the comfortable supply of all the people, and if it was all consumed in the country, there would necessarily, a much more equal division of this product take place. But as a part of the people depend on foreign nations, to consume the product of their labour, they are in a great measure, at the mercy of these nations. They may consume their produce, or not, as pleases them best. In proportion, as foreign nations stop consuming British manufactures, in that proportion must British subjects be deprived of the means of procuring the necessaries of life.

These are not, however, the only advantages arising from a monopoly of the home market. As such a market tends to augment the quantity of national industry, and of course national wealth, it also tends to make the people more habitually industrious; and habits of industry constitute a portion of national wealth. A man, who is industrious from habit, has a greater capacity for acquiring the necessaries and comforts of life, than one in similar circumstances, with idle habits: so of a nation.

A monopoly of the home market, has the effect of increasing a nation's skill in the arts and sciences, because it affords a motive for improvement in them. Improvement in the arts and sciences, is as effectual a mode of increasing the capacity of a nation, for acquiring the necessaries and comforts of life, as improvement in the cultivation of its land. A skillful mechanic has a greater capacity for acquiring the necessaries and comforts of life, than a man of equal strength, without any mechanic art. A nation, thoroughly skilled in all the arts, possesses a more inexhaustible source of national wealth, than if it possessed mountains of gold; and it would be much better economy for a nation, to impose heavy taxes for the purpose of acquiring such a source of wealth, than for conquering provinces, containing mountains of gold.

That is a miserable short-sighted policy, in private economy, and much more so in public, which looks only to the present, and disregards the future — it is killing the goose to get the golden egg. In private life, we look upon him as a wise man, who subjects himself to present privations and hardships, with a view to an ultimate benefit which shall overbalance the hardships. It is accounted wise, for a man, in his youth, to labour hard, and fare hard, that he may enjoy the good things of this life, more abundantly in old age. It is accounted wise for a man to go to great expense in clearing his lands, in building houses, mills, making roads and bridges, with a view to a future augmented product of the necessaries and comforts of life. It is accounted wise for a man to spend many years as an apprentice, to learn a trade, which may be a source of wealth in after life. This he does, to increase his capacity for acquiring the necessaries and comforts of life. "What is wise and prudent in the conduct of every private man, can scarce be folly in that of a great kingdom," says Dr. Smith.

It may be, and often is folly in a legislator, not to be longer-sighted in his schemes, than the wisest private individual. The schemes of the latter can only be adapted to the probable duration of his life, which can only be for a few years at most. The schemes of the former, may be adapted to the life of the nation, to which no limit can be fixed. Upon the same principle then, that it is wise for an individual to make calculations, and adopt measures, which look ten or twenty years ahead, it may be wise for a legislator to adopt measures, which look centuries ahead. Although it may be more beneficial for the time being, for a nation to import, than to manufacture its own comforts of life, still that ought not to decide the question. The inquiry should be made, how will it be fifty years hence? Admitting, that for the first five years, domestic manufactures may come at double price, still, if in ten, they will come at single price, and in twenty, at half price, we may be very sure that the present extra cost, is money well laid out for the nation, more especially, when it is considered that the annual product of labour cannot be accumulated, but must be annually consumed.

Although a high protecting duty may therefore prevent an individual from enjoying so great a portion of the comforts and luxuries of life, as he might otherwise do, or prevent him from accumulating so much private wealth, still national wealth is not thereby in the least degree diminished at any time.

From this it is not to be inferred that in all cases it would be advisable for government to secure to its own citizens the monopoly of the home trade, either by absolute prohibition of foreign importation, or by high protecting duties. All measures upon this subject should be regulated according to the existing circumstances of the nation; and the first thing to be ascertained, is, whether the nation has full employment in its ordinary occupations, or whether the sum of national industry is likely to be augmented by such a measure. A great deal of mischief may be done by an imprudent restriction upon the freedom of trade — it may have the effect to diminish the consumption of the country, which will paralize, instead of invigorating, industry. But when the people of a nation have not full employment, and a measure of this description will have the effect to give employment to a portion of them, it will promote the general prosperity of the country, and augment national wealth, although it may be adverse to individual interests. . . .

Thomas R. Dew: THE RESTRICTIVE SYSTEM

I will now proceed to another argument, much relied on by the advocates of the protecting system. In the free intercourse with foreign nations, they represent foreign industry as waging a war of competition with domestic industry and frequently supplanting it on its own soil. The interference of the legislator who shuts out these products from our market, appears like the act of a patriotic and kind friend who gives the wanted encouragement to domestic industry, and humanely prevents the payment of tribute to a for-

eign country. This cry about the encouragement of domestic industry, without any shadow of foundation for its justification, and the extreme plausibility which it seems to exhibit at first view, with the manifest absurdity which it is found to involve on closer scrutiny, will strikingly exemplify the sagacious remark of David Hume, that there are no subjects on which the first impressions of men are so liable to be false as in political matters.

First, then, we may be sure there is something false in this argument, for it

Thomas R. Dew, *Lectures on the Restrictive System* (Richmond: Samuel Shepherd & Co., 1829), pp. 114–126.

might with equal propriety be urged by either of the trading nations. America, for example, says to England, we will not take your woollens and cottons, for thereby we encourage your industry and discourage ours. Might not England, with equal propriety, answer, we will not take your cotton, tobacco, and even specie, for thereby we encourage your domestic industry, and likewise the industry of South America, and discourage our own. Might not the inference be at once drawn, from these very arguments, that each gained at least as much as it lost?

But, secondly, the source of the error is easily detected; it consists in not reflecting, that products can only be bought by means of products; that not one single dollar's worth of foreign produce will be sent to this country without an equivalent being given in exchange; that the raising or purchasing of this equivalent, encourages domestic industry much more efficiently than if we attempted to raise at home the manufacture instead of the equivalent; for, by the former plan we employ our industry in the most economical and productive manner, as I have already proved, and can get with equal labor, a greater quantity of manufactures than by the latter. I cannot better illustrate this subject for you, than by a pleasing and very simple illustration, furnished us by the editor of the Free Trade Advocate: "Tell me which weighs most, that pen-knife or those three silver half dollars," said a gentleman to us the other day. I took them in my hands, and pronounced them to be of equal weight. "That pen-knife," said my friend, "was made in Pittsburg. It cost me $1.50, and is the product of American industry; which, you see, has given to a little piece of iron and a small piece of a buck's horn, a value equal to its own weight in silver." All the company present were struck with this apparently

irresistible argument in favor of the American System. That iron ore and horn should be made as valuable as silver, by domestic industry, seemed almost incredible; and yet, the veracity of the owner of the pen-knife admitted no doubt on the subject. Could there be any question as to the benefit which the nation would derive from making its own pen-knives? seemed to be asked by several of the listeners. To meet this cogent fact, which to my friend was so conclusive, as to the soundness of the restrictive policy, that he proposed to burn the books on Political Economy, Adam Smith and all, I also resorted to a fact. I took out of my pocket an English pen-knife of the same weight as the American one, which had also cost a dollar and a half, and having the two before me, expressed myself somewhat in the following language:

"In the Pittsburg knife, I see the representative of a certain portion of American industry. I see the product of the labor of the hunter, the miner, the coal heaver, the smelter, the waggoner, the iron master, the steel maker and the cutler. I see that the knife is the result of the combined labor of these, and perhaps many others; and I also see the knife has cost what is precisely equal to the wages of a man for three days, estimating this at 50 cents per day. In other words, I see that in order that the nation should possess that pen-knife, one man must labor for three days. Now, in the English knife I also see a portion of American industry. I see in it the product of the labor of the ploughman, the sower, the reaper, the thresher, the miller, the woodcutter, the cooper, the waggoner, the factor, the merchant, the shipbuilder, the rigger, the sailmaker, the ship-smith, the ship-joiner, the plumber, the drayman, the stevidore, the mariner, and a dozen others, who are employed in producing wheat, converting it into flour, and in transporting it abroad. All this is American industry, *and is only another mode of making a pen-knife.* It has, however, the advantage over the first mode. If it were not for the protecting duty, the English knife would cost but one dollar, or in other words, the nation could procure it by the labor of one man for two days, instead of three; and if it is the interest of every individual that he should procure what he wants with the least possible quantity of labor, so must it be for the interest of all individuals, that is the nation."*

But, say the restrictionists, all this will do very well, as long as we exchange the products of our own labour for the products of other countries; but these, they will not always take, then we are obliged to pay in gold and silver, which are not produced in the United States. Grant it: But is it not evident that this gold and silver must be brought here before we can send it abroad; and is it not farther evident that it must have been purchased directly or indirectly with the products of domestic industry: for, we may be well assured that no nations in South America, or elsewhere, furnished them to us without an equivalent? If they had, however, it would only have been so much the better for the United States. The production of this equivalent, and the several exchanges made through its influence, encouraged domestic industry just as extensively, and even more so, than if the nation should attempt to make the products thus imported, directly by means of domestic industry.

But the restrictionists farther say, that the encouragement of domestic manufactures adds a new trade or employment to those already in use, and consequently leaves the labourer a greater choice of

* See Free Trade Advocate, No. 15, pp. 238–9, vol. 1.

trades. To this I answer, that he had always the choice of entering into this business, along with the capitalist, but the reason why they did not, was, they could more advantageously follow some other occupation. To make the advantages of this new trade equal to those of the old, all the consumers, of whom the labouring classes of society form the largest portion, must be taxed; so that we shall find the labourers and capitalists generally to pay exorbitantly for this choice of trades. No labourer, who had now a choice of three trades, in either of which he could get $1 per diem, would thank government for adding a fourth, and consequently increasing the range of his choice, but yet virtually decreeing that he should get only 90 cents per diem for his labour in either, instead of the dollar which he formerly got. This is truly giving him a choice with a vengeance. And thus will it always be found, that when government attempts to encourage domestic industry, it can only effect it by an imposition upon all orders of society generally, or upon some particular classes: in the first instance, the encouragement amounts in fact to a general discouragement; in the second, there is a glaring injustice on the part of government in benefitting one portion of society at the expense of another.

I cannot better expose the entire absurdity of this whole doctrine of encouraging domestic industry, than by quoting an ironical communication made to the Editor of the Free Trade Advocate, (whose valuable Journal has already been so often referred to in my investigations on this subject.) "Mr. Editor," says his correspondent, "the very heavy fall of snow which took place in this city on the 20th inst. (February,) afforded much delight to me and to many other friends of the 'American System,' on account of the great quantity of American industry it set in motion. Hundreds of labourers, who, owing to the stoppage of the navigation by ice, could not procure employment, were enabled to earn from 25 cents to $1 per day, by clearing away the snow from the pavements before people's doors. As I walked through the streets and saw the busy throng, I could not but felicitate myself upon the prosperity of my native city, Philadelphia at having such a great proportion of her labouring population employed. This activity appeared to me to be precisely similar to that which I had sometimes seen in a manufacturing village, where all was life and activity; and I could not but think a snow storm as far as it goes, is as beneficial as a tariff, by the employment it gives to the labouring poor. Thinks I, if falls of snow could only be brought about by an ordinance of the city councils, so as to afford a steady and constant protection to that industrious class of labourers, the snow-shovellers, the wealth of the city would increase to an astonishing degree, and we should soon have the balance of trade in our favor."*. . .

Let us suppose, that all the trades of society were in reality overdone: that labour and capital both were crowded into them to such a degree, that they had all ceased to be profitable. Then I say, if this were the case, and there were any new trades and employments, which could uplift the condition of the nation, these would be introduced at once, without government interference. For, if the old trades should in reality be overdone, all the labourers and capitalists must either remain in the old employments, depressed as they are, or they must commence some new business. If they continued in the same business, the competition among the capitalists would be so great as to reduce profits to a *minimum;*

* See Free Trade Advocate, vol. 1, No. 9, p. 139.

and the labourers would be so numerous in proportion to the work to be done, that the wages of labour would barely be sufficient for the support of human existence. This posture of affairs would most certainly induce a portion of labour and a portion of capital to quit these sinking trades, and betake themselves to some others, which would hold out fairer prospects. This would be a most propitious season too, for the introduction of manufactures; for, wages would now be extremely low, and profits at a *minimum*. And we have seen, that these are the principal elements of the cost of production. Our country could, under these circumstances, compete with Great Britain, or any other nation, in manufacturing, and no law would be necessary to effect it.

But we will illustrate this in another manner. We have already seen, in the course of our lectures on the restrictive system, that the principle which leads to the exchange of commodities between nation and nation, is this: That one nation, by devoting its labour and capital to certain employments, and exchanging the products of those for other products, can, by this means, get more of the latter, than if it attempted to make them directly. Thus, the Virginia farmer finds, perhaps, that one year's labour in agriculture, would exchange for as many manufactures as would require two years' labour to produce them at home. He therefore finds it cheapest to get his manufactures from abroad. Now, let us suppose agriculture to be growing less and less profitable, until it is finally overdone, and see what will be the result. Suppose agricultural products to decline in price, till the farmer can exchange one year's labour for only as many manufactures as would require 1½ years of domestic labour: he would find agriculture much less profitable than formerly, but still more advantageous, by 50 per cent., than manufacturing. The farmer, at this stage of depression, would repine and murmur at the decline of prices. He would say the business was overdone, and he would charge his calamities, perhaps, to this circumstance: hard times and scarcity of money, would be the universal theme among the farmers; yet none would quit the business of agriculture for manufactures; for this would be to pass from the confines of Scylla, into the actual whirlpool of Charybdis.

Let us suppose the business still farther to decline, so that one year's agricultural labour will only procure for the farmer as much manufactured produce as would require 1¼ years to produce it at home: still he would sing the tale of his calamities, cast a lingering, longing look back to the times when he almost got double the quantity which he now gets for his produce. Yet, he would not give up his business and go to manufacturing, for still his declining trade, with all its disadvantages, is 25 per cent. better than manufactures.

But this career of agricultural depression, we will suppose, stops not here; but continues till the farmer finds that for one year's labour in agriculture, he only gets manufactures that would require the same labour to procure them here. Then would we see manufactures springing up around us, the enterprise and restless activity of capitalists and labourers would quickly explore these new channels of industry, and every successive depression in agriculture would give additional vigour to manufactures, until we could even undersell the English in foreign countries. . . .

But, say the advocates of prohibitory measures, a nation may be prepared for manufactures, but such is the prejudice in favor of old employments, that labor

and capital will not desert them to go to the new. After what has already been said on this point, I shall be very brief. In the first place, then, I would say, that even granting that men were not disposed to quit their old employments till they sunk greatly below the general level, yet would tampering be extremely hazardous, for it might begin too soon. One manufacture might be successfully introduced into the country, while hundreds of others might be forced upon the nation, without being competent to manufacture them as cheaply as foreign nations.

Thus taking our own country, perhaps the legislator might be successful in introducing the manufacture of coarse cotton goods as cheap as they could be procured abroad. But, for want of proper knowledge, he introduces in the same way, woollens, iron, hemp, molasses, and a long list, all of which may be produced in the country before their time. These, then, entail a lasting calamity upon the nation. Would it not, therefore, be wisdom to run the risk of introducing coarse cottons a little too late, than to bring all these evils in their train?

But I deny altogether this complete indisposition to enter into new employments, which is supposed to exist in our country. I know, generally speaking, that those engaged in trade, will, with equal advantages, or even with something less than equality, prefer remaining in the old trades. Individual interest prompts to this preference, and consequently the good of the nation is promoted by it, because the individual is better qualified for it, and his superiority of qualification for this business, may make up in his particular case, for superiority of profit in some other, and therefore he will not quit it. But there are capitalists constantly in the community, who have not yet chosen their employments, and labourers just arrived at manhood, who are not yet wedded to any particular species of human industry. Interest will most assuredly prompt these into the most lucrative employments; and where all are equally lucrative, difference of capacity, inclination, &c. will cause all to be filled: and the manufacturing business will be sure to come in for its due share of labour and capital. And let me not be told there is a want of energy in our country. Energy and enterprise will always be found wherever there is liberty. And where, I would ask, is the nation that enjoys the freedom of America? When we walk abroad, we are as free as the air that encircles us. The fullest scope is here furnished for the complete development of all our faculties and inclinations. . . .

But, let us proceed more particularly to the consideration of the argument drawn from the fluctuation and insecurity of the foreign market. And first, I would observe, that the foreign market is, generally speaking, much less fluctuating than the home market, if you throw out of view the consideration of wars.

1st. The foreign market being more extensive generally than the home market, is much less affected by increased or diminished supplies from any one nation. Every increase of water flowing into the James River above its tides, swells this river, and renders the augmentation of volume visible to the eye. But this noble river, when it empties its waters into the Atlantic, produces no appreciable effect on that great reservoir of waters. So, the slightest augmentation or diminution of supply, will produce a visible effect on the home market, when a small one; whereas, the foreign market will scarcely feel the effects, in consequence of its vast extent.

But, 2dly. The foreign market is less liable to fluctuation than the home, both with regard to buying and selling; because it is extremely improbable that years of abundance or of scarcity, of augmentation or diminution of supply, should occur in many different countries at the same time. The excess in one counteracts the deficiency in another. France may produce this year as much as her wants require, of a particular commodity, which she generally purchases of us, but Spain and Italy may be deficient, and thus the price remains equable. So, there may be luxuriant harvests in the United States, and a consequent excess in production; but there may be bad seasons in South America and England, and a diminished supply consequent on them. The produce of the United States may thus still maintain one equable undeviating price. And the farmer, in this state of things, would never deprecate the bounty of Heaven, in sending the most genial seasons, and the most abundant crops. . . .

VI   LATER APPRAISALS

D. G. Harriman: THE BENEFITS OF PROTECTION

. . . At the close of the war between the United States and Great Britain, England and English manufacturers made two discoveries which were very startling and disagreeable to them. First, That having been deprived by the Embargo Act and the subsequent war of the American markets, the British manufacturers found their warehouses at the close of the war full to bursting with unsold productions of various kinds, for which they were very anxious, but unable, to find a market. Second, That the Americans compelled by the same reasons to rely upon themselves instead of the English manufacturers for their supplies during this period, had established successfully a large number of home industries, and were, by this means, able to a great degree to supply their own market.

In this dilemma, England saw that she must act promptly and crush out these young American industries, or her American market would be forever lost, and her manufacturing industries permanently crippled. So she resolved to flood this country with her goods then on hand, many of which were old and out of fashion, far below cost. It was a matter of so much importance that it' was discussed in Parliament, and Mr. (afterward Lord) Brougham declared in the House of Commons in 1816: "It is well worth while to incur a loss upon the first exportation, in order, by the glut, to stifle in the

cradle those infant manufactures in the United States, which the war has forced into existence."

This policy was decided upon, and Great Britain poured her fabrics and acculmulated [sic] stocks of goods into our markets in an overwhelming torrent and far below cost. The tariff of 1816 was intended as a barrier against this inundation, and under ordinary circumstances would have proved such. But it was a matter of life or death with the English manufacturers, and so they continued to pour in their goods upon us at prices far lower than we could make them; and true to British custom they perservered [sic] in this policy till our own industries were very nearly ruined.

The foreign goods imported at this period were more than twice the quantity that could be consumed. Niles, in his history, says: "It is notorious that great sums of money were expended by the British to destroy our flocks of sheep, that they might thereby ruin our manufactories. They bought up and immediately slaughtered great numbers of sheep; they bought our best machinery and sent it off to England, and hired our best mechanics and most skillful workmen to go to England, simply to get them out of this country, and so hinder and destroy our existing and prospective manufactures."

RESULTS OF THE REPEAL. — Then great depression in all branches of busi-

D. G. Harriman, *American Tariffs from Plymouth Rock to McKinley, A Complete and Impartial History* (New York: The American Protective Tariff League, 1892), pp. 23–27.

ness at once followed. Bankruptcy soon became general, and financial ruin was everywhere present. It could not be otherwise. Carey, Greeley, Clay, Benton and others show that this was one of the most distressful periods of our national existence. "No price for property; no sales except those of the sheriff and the marshal; no purchasers at execution sales except the creditor, or some hoarder of money; no employment for industry; no demand for labor; no sale for the products of the farm; no sound of the hammer, except that of the auctioneer knocking down property. Distress was the universal cry of the people; relief, the universal demand, was thundered at the doors of all Legislatures, State and Federal." (Benton).

Horace Greeley says of this period: "At the close of the second war with England, Peace found this country dotted with furnaces and factories which had sprung up under the precarious shelter of embargo and war. These not yet firmly established found themselves suddenly exposed to a relentless and determined foreign competition. Great Britain poured her fabrics, far below cost, upon our markets in a perfect deluge. Our manufactures went down like grass before the mower, and our agriculture and the wages of labor speedily followed. Financial prostration was general, and the presence of debt was universal. In New England, fully one-fourth of the property went through the sheriff's mill, and the prostration was scarcely less general elsewhere. In Kentucky the presence of debt was simply intolerable. In New York, the leading merchants, in 1817, united in a memorial to Congress to save our commerce as well as our manufactures from utter ruin, by increasing the tariff duties."

Henry Clay declared that the average depression in the value of property, under that state of things, was not less than fifty per cent.

1818. – THE TARIFF ACT OF 1818 was simply an amendment by which tariff duty was imposed upon a few articles which, prior thereto, were free.

It thus appears that the Tariff Acts of 1816 and 1818 were no exception to the rule that protective tariffs conduce to national prosperity, and very low tariff rates to national adversity; for though they were "moderately protective," in name, yet, under the outrageous and disgracefully selfish policy of Great Britain – a policy which we could not then have anticipated – those tariffs afforded insufficient protection; and insufficient protection is, practically, as bad as tariff for revenue only.

Second Protection Period – 1824–1833

1824. – PROTECTION AGAIN RESTORED. – The disastrous state of affairs described in Chapter III. continued for several years, until our people, with a mighty effort, resolved to endure it no longer; and in 1824 Congress gave us a new tariff, far in advance of that of 1789, and our first protective tariff that gave us real protection.

This tariff was passed in response to a general demand of the country; and upon the urgent recommendation of President Monroe to give "additional protection to those articles which we are prepared to manufacture," etc. Everybody, except a few free traders, had become disgusted with a tariff that was nominally "moderately protective," while in fact, it afforded no real protection; and the Congress of that year was largely in favor of a strong protective tariff, in fact as well as in name.

The advocates of this Tariff Act insisted upon its passage, in order to give to the country that strength and power which arise from possessing within itself the means of defense, and to rescue it from the dangers and disgrace of habitual dependence upon foreign nations for the common daily necessaries of life.

The enemies of the bill were no less determined in their opposition. No denunciation of it could be too severe; no prophecy of evil to come from it could be too doleful.

Soon after the tariff bill of 1824 was reported, a New York evening newspaper, now, as then, one of the ablest and most uncompromising advocates of free trade, said, editorially:

"Pass the tariff as reported by the committee and you palsy the Nation. Pass it, and where will you any longer find occupants for your costly piles of stores and dwelling-houses? Pass it, and who will be exempt from its grinding operation?

"The poorer classes, especially, must feel its effect in paying an additional price for every article of clothing they and their families wear, and every mouthful they eat or drink, save cold water; and to that will they ere long be reduced."— New York *Evening Post*, July, 1824.

Major McKinley commenting on this, says: "None of these awful prophecies were fulfilled; none of these dire results ensued. The nation was not palsied, but quickened into new life. The merchants did not move out of their costly piles of stores and dwelling-houses, they remained only to require larger and finer and more costly ones; the poorer classes were not driven to cold water as their only food and diet, but their labor was in greater demand and their wages advanced in price. The entire country under the tariff moved on to higher triumphs in industrial progress, and to a higher and better destiny for all of its people."

John Randolph, one of the ablest of Democrats, fiercely opposed the bill, and in a speech in Congress, after showing the great advantages of Great Britain in manufacturing, added: "It is in such a climate only that the human animal can bear, without extirpation, the corrupted air, the noisome exhalations, the incessant labor of these accursed manufactories. Yes, sir, accursed, for I say it is an accursed thing. We should have the yellow fever from June to January, and January to June. The climate of this country alone, were there no other natural obstacles to it, says aloud — You shall not manufacture."

One of its strongest advocates and supporters was Andrew Jackson, then United States Senator, and now the patron saint of the Democratic Party. Let us see what he thought of protection in 1824: "Providence," said he, "has filled our mountains and our plains with minerals — with lead, iron and copper — and given us a climate and soil for the growing of hemp and wool. These being the greatest materials of our national defense, they ought to have extended to them adequate and fair protection, that our manufacturers and laborers may be placed in a fair competition with those of Europe; and that we may have within our country a supply of those leading and important articles so essential in war. We have been too long subject to the policy of British merchants. It is time we should become a little more Americanized; and, instead of feeding the paupers and laborers of England, feed our own; or else in a short time by continuing our present policy (that under tariff of 1816) we shall all be rendered paupers ourselves. It is my opinion therefore that a careful and judicious tariff is much wanted."

RESULTS QUICK AND HELPFUL. — The Bill was passed, and again, and at once, an era of great financial prosperity set in. So marked and helpful was the improvement that in 1828 the duties were raised still higher; and yet business improved; new industries were started, and prosperity gladdened the people.

Hear what President Andrew Jackson said in his annual message, in December, 1832, concerning the results and benefits of eight years of protection under the Tariffs of 1824 and 1828: "Our country presents, on every side, marks of prosperity and happiness, unequalled, perhaps, in any other portion of the world."

The relief to the country, attained through these Tariffs of 1824 and 1828, "was profound and general, reaching all classes — the farmer, the manufacturer, the ship-owner, the mechanic, and the day laborer. The change was as great as was wrought when Hamilton smote the rock of public credit and abundant streams of revenue gushed forth." (Webster.)

Henry Clay, speaking in the United States Senate in 1832 about this period, said: "On a general survey we behold cultivation extended; the arts flourishing; the face of the country improved; our people fully and profitably employed; the public countenance exhibiting tranquility, contentment and happiness; its public debt of two wars nearly redeemed; and, to crown all, the public treasury overflowing. If the term of seven years were to be selected of the greatest prosperity which this people has enjoyed since the establishment of their present Constitution, it would be exactly that period of seven years which immediately followed the passage of the Tariff of 1824."

This view is sustained by the best writers concerning that period, who all agree that our manufactures were flourishing, that our currency was good, our crops abundant, and our commerce prosperous. These combined influences in-

variably enhance the demand for labor, increase its value, establish a general prosperity for the country and contentment for the people.

President John Quincy Adams, who succeeded Mr. Monroe, was also a strong friend of protection, and in his fourth annual message discusses at some length our agricultural, commercial and manufacturing interests, and shows that "all these interests are alike under the protecting power of the legislative authority," and proceeds to make himself clear and explicit in his defense of the principles of protection.

1832.—TARIFF OF 1828 AMENDED. — The Tariff Act of 1832 was really nothing but some slight amendments to the Act of 1828. Southern feeling against the Tariff of 1828 was exceedingly bitter, and they were determined to have actual free trade, if possible. They demanded, through the Committee of Ways and Means, that the protective system be "utterly and absolutely abandoned;" and declared that "congress should adopt no half-way measures, no temporary expedients, but 'reform it altogether.'"

But the country, as a whole, had never been so prosperous as under the policy of the Tariff of 1828, and they were in no mood to yield to this foolish demand of the South. But, for the sake of peace and of conciliating the South, they were willing to make some concessions to this free trade prejudice, and, therefore, certain coarse wools were put upon the free list, and some reduction was granted upon articles made from those wools. But the protective principle of the Act of 1828 was still retained on the expressed ground that it was necessary for building up and sustaining our own manufactures as one of the essential means of increasing and maintaining our national greatness.

The Cotton Manufacture

When . . . the period of restriction began, in 1808, the importation of foreign [cotton] goods was first impeded, and soon entirely prevented. The domestic manufacture accordingly extended with prodigious rapidity. Already during the years 1804–8 greater activity must have prevailed; for in the latter year fifteen mills had been built, running 8,000 spindles. In 1809 the number of mills built shot up to 62, with 31,000 spindles, and while 25 more mills were in course of erection. In 1812 there were 50 factories within thirty miles of Providence, operating nearly 60,000 spindles, and capable of operating 100,000. During the war the same rapid growth continued, rendered possible as it was by the increasing supply of raw cotton from the South. The number of spindles was said to be 80,000 in 1811, and 500,000 in 1815. In 1800, 500 bales of cotton had been used; in 1805, 1,000 bales. In 1810 the number consumed rose to 10,000; in 1815, it was 90,000. These figures cannot be supposed to be at all accurate; but they indicate clearly an enormously rapid development of the manufacture of cotton.

The machinery in almost all these new factories was for spinning yarn only. Weaving was still carried on by the hand-loom, usually by weavers working in considerable numbers on account for manufacturers. Toward the end of the war, however, a change began to be made almost as important in the history of textile manufactures as the use of the spinning-jenny and mule: namely, the substitution of the power-loom for the hand-loom. The introduction of the power-loom took place in England at about the same time, and some intimation of its use seems to have reached the inventor in this country, Francis C. Lowell. He perfected the machine, however, without any use of English models, in the course of the year 1814. In the same year it was put in operation at a factory at Waltham, Mass. There for the first time the entire process of converting cotton into cloth took place under one roof. The last important step in giving textile manufactures their present form was thus taken.

When peace was made in 1815, and imports began again, the newly established factories, most of which were badly equipped and loosely managed, met with serious embarrassment. Many were entirely abandoned. The manufacturers petitioned Congress for assistance; and they received, in 1816, that measure of help which the public was then disposed to grant. The tariff of 1816 levied a duty of 25 per cent. on cotton goods for three years, a duty considered sufficiently protective in those days of inexperience in protective legislation. At the same time it was provided that all cotton cloths, costing less than 25 cents a yard, should be considered to have cost 25 cents and be charged with duty accordingly; that is, should be charged 25 per cent. of 25 cents, or 6¼ cents a yard, whatever their real value or cost. This was the first of the minimum valuation provisos which played so considerable a part in later tariff legislation, and which have been maintained in large part to the present time. A similar minimum duty was imposed on cotton-yarns. At the time when these measures were passed, the minimum provisos

From F. W. Taussig, *The Tariff History of the United States* (New York: G. P. Putnam's Sons, 1892).

hardly served to increase appreciably the weight of the duty of 25 per cent. Coarse cotton cloths were then worth from 25 cents to 30 cents, and, even without the provisos, would have paid little, if any thing, less than the minimum duty. But, after 1818, the use of the power-loom, and the fall in the price of raw cotton, combined greatly to reduce the prices of cotton goods. The price of çoarse cottons fell to 19 cents in 1819, 13 cents in 1826, and 8½ cents in 1829. The minimum duty became proportionately heavier as the price decreased, and, in a few years after its enactment, had become prohibitive of the importation of the coarser kinds of cotton cloths.

During the years immediately after the war, the aid given in the tariff of 1816 was not sufficient to prevent severe depression in the cotton manufacture. Reference has already been made to the disadvantages which, under the circumstances of the years 1815–18, existed for all manufacturers who had to meet competition from abroad. But when the crisis of 1818–19 had brought about a rearrangement of prices more advantageous for manufacturers, matters began to mend. The minimum duty became more effective in handicapping foreign competitors. At the same time the power-loom was generally introduced. Looms made after an English model were introduced in the factories of Rhode Island, the first going into operation in 1817; while in Massachusetts and New Hampshire the loom invented by Lowell was generally adopted after 1816. From these various causes the manufacture soon became profitable. There is abundant evidence to show that shortly after the crisis the cotton manufacture had fully recovered from the depression that followed the war. The profits made were such as to cause a rapid extension of the industry. The beginning of those

manufacturing villages which now form the characteristic economic feature of New England falls in this period. Nashua was founded in 1823. Fall River, which had grown into some importance during the war of 1814, grew rapidly from 1820 to 1830. By far the most important and the best known of the new ventures in cotton manufacturing was the foundation of the town of Lowell, which was undertaken by the same persons who had been engaged in the establishment of the first power-loom factory at Waltham. The new town was named after the inventor of the power-loom. The scheme of utilizing the falls of the Merrimac, at the point where Lowell now stands, had been suggested as early as 1821, and in the following year the Merrimac Manufacturing Company was incorporated. In 1823 manufacturing began, and was profitable from the beginning; and in 1824 the future growth of Lowell was clearly foreseen.

From this sketch of the early history of the cotton manufacture we may draw some conclusions. Before 1808 the difficulties in the way of the introduction of this branch of industry were such that it made little progress. These difficulties were largely artificial; and though the obstacles arising from ignorance of the new processes and from the absence of experienced workmen, were partly removed by the appearance of Slater, they were sufficient, when combined with the stimulus which the condition of foreign trade gave to agriculture and the carrying trade, to prevent any appreciable development. Had this period come to an end without any accompanying political change — had there been no embargo, no non-intercourse act, and no war with England — the growth of the cotton manufacture, however certain to have taken place in the end, might have been subject to much friction and loss. Conjecture as to what might have been is dangerous, especially in economic history, but it seems reasonable to suppose that if the period before 1808 had come to an end without a jar, the eager competition of well-established English manufacturers, the lack of familiarity with the processes, and the long-continued habit, especially in New England, of almost exclusive attention to agriculture, commerce, and the carrying trade, might have rendered slow and difficult the change, however inevitable it may have been, to greater attention to manufactures. Under such circumstances there might have been room for the legitimate application of protection to the cotton manufacture as a young industry. But this period, in fact, came to an end with a violent shock, which threw industry out of its accustomed grooves, and caused the striking growth of the cotton manufacture from 1808 to 1815. The transition caused much suffering, but it took place sharply and quickly. The interruption of trade was equivalent to a rude but vigorous application of protection, which did its work thoroughly. When peace came, in 1815, it found a large number of persons and a great amount of capital engaged in the cotton manufacture, and the new processes of manufacture introduced on an extensive scale. Under such circumstances the industry was certain to be maintained if it was for the economic interest of the country that it should be carried on.

The duties of the tariff of 1816, therefore, can hardly be said to have been necessary. Nevertheless, they may have been of service. The assistance they gave was, it is true, insignificant in comparison with the shelter from all foreign competition during the war. Indeed, most manufacturers desired much higher duties than were granted. It is true, also, that the minimum duty on cottons was least effective during the years immediately after the war, when the price of cottons was higher, and the duty was therefore proportionately less high. But these years between the close of the war and the general fall of prices in 1819 were trying for the manufacturers. The normal economic state, more favorable for them, was not reached till the crisis of 1818–19 was well over. During the intervening years the minimum duty may have assisted the manufacturers without causing any permanent charge on the people. The fact that careful and self-reliant men, like the founders of the Waltham and Lowell enterprises, were most urgent in advising the adoption of the rates of 1816 — at a time, too, when the practice of appealing to Congress for assistance when in distress had not yet become common among manufacturers — may indicate that those rates were of service in encouraging the continuance of the manufacture. How seriously its progress would have been impeded or retarded by the absence of duties, cannot be said. On the whole, although the great impulse to the industry was given during the war, the duties on cottons in the tariff of 1816 may be considered a judicious application of the principle of protection to young industries.

Before 1824, the manufacture, as we have seen, was securely established. The further application of protection in that and in the following years was needless, and, so far as it had any effect, was harmful. The minimum valuation was raised in 1824 to 30 cents, and in 1828 to 35 cents. The minimum duties were thereby raised to 7½ and 8¾ cents respectively. By 1824 the manufacture had so firm a hold that its further extension should have been left to individual enterprise, which by that time might have been relied on to carry the industry as far as it was for the economic interest of the country that it should be carried. . . .

The Woollen Manufacture

The sudden and striking growth of the cotton manufacture in the last hundred years has caused its history, in this country as in others, to be written with comparative fulness. Of the early history of the manufacture of woollen goods in the United States we have but scanty accounts; but these are sufficient to show that the general course of events was similar to that in cotton manufacturing. During the colonial period and the years immediately after the Revolution, such woollen cloths as were not spun and woven in households for personal use were imported from England. The goods of household manufacture, however, formed, and for many years after the introduction of machinery continued to form, by far the greater part of those in use. The first attempt at making woollens in large quantities is said to have been made at Ipswich, Mass., in 1792; but no machinery seems to have been used in this undertaking. In 1794 the new machinery was for the first time applied to the manufacture of wool, and it is noteworthy that, as in the case of the cotton manufacture, the machinery was introduced by English workmen. These were the brothers Arthur and John Scholfield, who came to the United States in 1793, and in the next year established a factory at Byfield, Mass. Their machinery, however, was exclusively for carding wool, and for dressing (fulling) woollen goods; and for the latter purpose it was probably in no way different from that of the numerous fulling-mills which were scattered over the country during colonial times. Spinning and weaving were done, as before, on the spinning-wheel and the hand-loom. The Scholfields introduced carding-machinery in place of the hand-cards, and seem to have carried on their business in several places with success. A Scotchman, James Saunderson, who emigrated in 1794, also introduced carding-machines at New Ipswich, N. H., in 1801. Their example, however, was followed by few. Carding-machines were introduced in a few other places between 1800 and 1808; but no development of the business of systematically making cloth, or preparing wool for sale, took place. The application of machinery for spinning does not seem to have been made at all. One great difficulty in the way of the woollen manufacture was the deficient supply and poor quality of wool. The means of overcoming this were supplied when in 1802 a large flock of fine merino sheep was imported from Spain, followed in 1809 and 1810 by several thousand pure merinos from the same country. But imports from England continued to be large, and those woollen cloths that were not homespun were obtained almost exclusively from the mother country.

When the period of restriction began in 1808, the woollen manufacture received, like all other industries in the same position, a powerful stimulus. The prices of broadcloth, then the chief cloth worn besides homespun, rose enormously, as did those of flannels, blankets, and other goods, which had previously been obtained almost exclusively by importation. We have no such detailed statements as are given of the rise of the cotton manufacture. It is clear, however, that the manufacture of woollen goods, which had had no real existence before, began, and was considerably extended. The spinning of wool by machinery was introduced, and goods were made for sale on a large scale. As early as 1810 the carding and spinning of wool by machinery was begun in some of the cotton mills in Rhode

Island. In Northampton, Mass., Oriskany, N. Y., and other places, large establishments for the manufacture of woollen goods and of satinets (mixed cotton and woollen goods) sprang up. The value of woollen goods made in factories is said to have risen from $4,000,000 in 1810 to $19,000,000 in 1815.

After 1815 the makers of woollens naturally encountered great difficulties in face of the renewed and heavy importations of English goods. The tariff of 1816 gave them the same duty that was levied on cottons, 25 per cent., to be reduced in three years to 20 per cent. The reduction of the duty to 20 per cent., which was to have taken place in 1819, was then postponed, and in the end never took place. No minimum valuation was fixed for woollen goods; hence there was not, as for cotton goods, a minimum duty. Wool was admitted at a duty of 15 per cent. The scheme of duties, under the tariff of 1816, thus afforded no very vigorous protection. Nor did the provisions of the act of 1824 materially improve the position of the woollen manufacturers. The duty on woollen goods was in that act raised to 30 per cent. in the first instance, and to 33⅓ per cent. after 1825. At the same time the duty on wool (except that costing ten cents a pound or less) was raised to 20 per cent. in the first place, to 25 per cent. after 1825, and to 30 per cent. after 1826. If foreign wool had to be imported to supplement the domestic supply, — and such a necessity has constantly existed in this country since 1816, — the increased price of wool in this country, as compared with other countries which admitted wool free or at a lower duty, would tend to make the effectual protection to woollen manufacturers far from excessive.

Notwithstanding the very moderate encouragement given from 1816 to 1828, the woollen manufacture steadily progressed after the crisis of 1819, and in 1828 was securely established. During the years from the close of the war till 1819 much embarrassment was felt, and many establishments were given up; but others tided over this trying time. After 1819 the industry gradually responded to the more favorable influences which then set in for manufactures, and made good progress. During 1821 and 1822 large investments were made in factories for making woollen cloths, especially in New England. In 1823 the manufacturers of woollens in Boston were sufficiently numerous to form an independent organization for the promotion of their interests, which were, in that case, to secure higher protective duties. The best evidence which we have of the condition of the industry during these years is to be found in the testimony given in 1828 by various woollen manufacturers before the Committee of the House of Representatives on Manufactures. This testimony shows clearly that the industry was established in 1828 on such a scale that the difficulties arising from lack of skill and experience, unfamiliarity with machinery and methods, and other such temporary obstacles, no longer had influence in preventing its growth. The capital invested by the thirteen manufacturers who testified before this committee varied from $20,000 to $200,000, the average being $85,000. The quantity of wool used by each averaged about 62,000 pounds per year. These figures indicate a scale of operation very considerable for those days. Six of the factories referred to had been established between 1809 and 1815. With the possible exception of one, in regard to which the date of foundation was not stated, none had been established in the years between 1815 and 1820; the remaining six had been built after 1820. Spinning-machinery was in use in all. Some used power-looms, others hand-looms. The application of the power-loom to weaving woollens, said one manufacturer, had been made in the United States earlier than in England. An indication, similar to this, of the point reached by the American producers in the use of machinery, was afforded by the difference of opinion in regard to the comparative merits of the jenny, and of the "Brewster," a spinning-machine of recent invention. Goods of various kinds were made — broadcloths, cassimeres, flannels, satinets, and kerseys. The opinion was expressed by several that the mere cost of manufacturing was not greater in the United States than in England; that the American manufacturer could produce, at as low prices as the English, if he could obtain his wool at as low prices as his foreign competitor. This testimony seems to show conclusively that at the time when it was given the woollen manufacture had reached that point at which it might be left to sustain itself; at which accidental or artificial obstacles no longer stood in the way of its growth. That many of the manufacturers themselves wanted higher duties, is, for obvious reasons, not inconsistent with this conclusion. Progress had been less certain and rapid than in the case of the kindred cotton manufacture, for the conditions of production were less distinctly favorable. The displacement of the household products by those of the factory was necessarily a gradual process, and made the advance of the woollen manufacture normally more slow than that of the kindred industry. But the growth of the cotton manufacture, so similar to that of wool, of itself removed many of the obstacles arising from the recent origin of the latter. The use of machinery became common, and, when the first great steps had been taken, was

transferred with comparative ease from one branch of textile production to another. In 1828, when for the first time heavy protection was given by a complicated system of minimum duties, and when the actual rates rose, in some cases, to over 100 per cent., this aid was no longer needed to sustain the woollen manufacture. The period of youth had then been past.

It appears that direct protective legislation had even less influence in promoting the introduction and early growth of the woollen than of the cotton manufacture. The events of the period of restriction, from 1808 to 1815, led to the first introduction of the industry, and gave it the first strong impulse. Those events may indeed be considered to have been equivalent to effective, though crude and wasteful, protective legislation, and it may be that their effect, as compared with the absence of growth before 1808, shows that protection in some form was needed to stimulate the early growth of the woollen manufacture. But, by 1815, the work of establishing the manufacture had been done. The moderate duties of the period from 1816 to 1828, partly neutralized by the duties on wool, may have something to sustain it; but the position gained in 1815 would hardly have been lost in the absence of these duties. By 1828, when strong protection was first given, a secure position had certainly been reached.

The Iron Manufacture

We turn now to the early history of the iron manufacture, — the production of crude iron, pig and bar. We shall examine here the production, not of the finished article, but of the raw material. It is true that the production of crude iron takes place under somewhat different conditions from those which affect cotton and woollen goods. The production of pig-iron is more in the nature of an extractive industry, and, under ordinary circumstances, is subject in some degree to the law of diminishing returns. To commodities produced under the conditions of that law, the argument for protection to young industries has not been supposed, at least by its more moderate advocates, to apply, since the sites where production will be carried on to best advantage are apt to be determined by unalterable physical causes. It happens, however, that changes in the processes of production, analogous to those which took place in the textile industries, were made at about the same time in the manufacture of crude iron. These changes rendered more possible the successful application of the principle of protection to young industries, and make the discussion of its application more pertinent. There is another reason why we should consider, in this connection, the raw material rather than the finished article. The production of the latter, of the tools and implements made of iron, has not, in general, needed protection in this country, nor has protection often been asked for it. The various industries by which crude iron is worked into tools and consumable articles were firmly established already in the colonial period, and since then have maintained themselves with little difficulty. The controversy on the protection of the iron manufacture has been confined mainly to the production of pig- and bar-iron. It is to this, therefore, that we shall direct our attention. The production of pig- and bar-iron will be meant when, in the following pages the "iron manufacture" is spoken of.

During the eighteenth century England was a country importing, and not, as she is now, one exporting, crude iron. The production of pig- and bar-iron was accordingly encouraged in her colonies, and production was carried on in them to an extent considerable for those days. Large quantities of bar-iron were exported from the American colonies to England. The manufacture of iron was firmly established in the colonies according to the methods common at the time. During the second half of the eighteenth century, however, the great change took place in England in the production of iron which has placed that country in its present position among iron-making countries, and has exercised so important an influence on the material progress of our time. Up to that time charcoal had been used exclusively for smelting iron, and the iron manufacture had tended to fix itself in countries where wood was abundant, like Norway, Sweden, Russia, and the American colonies. About 1750 the use of coke in the blast furnace began. The means were thus given for producing iron in practically unlimited quantities, without dependence for fuel on forests easily exhaustible; and in the latter part of the century, when the steam-engine supplied the motive power for the necessary strong blast, production by means of coke increased with great rapidity. At the same time, in 1783 and 1784, came the inventions of Cort for puddling and rolling iron. By these the transformation of pig-iron into bar-iron of convenient sizes was effected in large quantities. Before the inventions of Cort, pig-iron had been first converted into bar under the hammer, and the bar, at a second distinct operation in a slitting mill, converted into bars and rods of convenient size. The rolled bar made by the processes of puddling and rolling — which are still in common use — is inferior in quality, at least after the first rolling, to the hammered and slit iron, known as hammered bar, produced by the old method. Cort's processes, however, made the iron much more easily and cheaply, and the lower price of the rolled iron more than compensated, for most purposes, for its inferior quality. At the same time these processes made easy and fostered the change from production on a small scale to production on a large scale. This tended to bring about still greater cheapness, and made the revolution in the production of iron as great as that in the textile industries, and similar to it in many important respects.

During the period 1789–1808 these changes in the iron manufacture were too recent to have had any appreciable effect on the conditions of production and supply in the United States. The manufacture of iron, and its transformation into implements of various kinds, went on without change from the methods of the colonial period. Pig-iron continued to be made and converted into hammered bar in small and scattered works and forges. No pig-iron seems to have been imported. Bar-iron was imported, in quantities not inconsiderable, from Russia; but no crude iron was imported from England. The importations of certain iron articles, not much advanced beyond the crude state, such as nails, spikes, anchors, cables, showed a perceptible increase during this period. Whether this increase was the result of the general conditions which tended to swell imports during this period, or was the first effect of the new position which England was taking as an iron-making country, cannot be determined. Information on the state of the industry during this period is meagre; but it seems to have been little affected by the protective duties which Congress enacted on nails, steel, and some other articles. No protection was attempted to be given to the production of pig or bar-iron, for it was thought that the domestic producers would be able to compete successfully

with their foreign competitors in this branch of the iron-trade.

During the period of restriction from 1808 to 1815, the iron and manufactures of iron previously imported, had to be obtained, as far as possible, at home. A large increase in the quantity of iron made in the country accordingly took place. The course of events was so similar to that already described in regard to textile manufactures that it need not be referred to at length. When peace came, there were unusually heavy importations of iron, prices fell rapidly, and the producers had to go through a period of severe depression.

In 1816 Congress was asked to extend protection to the manufacture of iron, as well as to other industries. The tariff of 1816 imposed a duty of 45 cents a hundred-weight on hammered-bar iron, and one of $1.50 a hundred-weight on rolled bar, with corresponding duties on sheet, hoop, and rod iron. Pig-iron was admitted under an *ad valorem* duty of 20 per cent. At the prices of bar-iron in 1816, the specific duty on hammered bar was equivalent to about 20 per cent., and was, therefore, but little higher than the rates of 15 and 17½ per cent. levied in 1804 and 1807. The duty on rolled bar was much higher, relatively to price, as well as absolutely, than that on hammered bar, and was the only one of the iron duties of 1816 which gave distinct and vigorous protection. These duties were not found sufficient to prevent the manufacturers from suffering heavy losses, and more effective protection was demanded. In 1818, Congress, by a special act, raised the duties on iron considerably, at the same time, as was noted above, that it postponed the reduction from 25 to 20 per cent. on the duty on cottons and woollens. Both of these measures were concessions to protective feeling, and they may have been the result of an uneasy consciousness of the disturbed state of the country and of the demand for protection which was to follow the financial crisis of the next year. The act of 1818 fixed the duty on pig-iron at 50 cents per hundred-weight — the first specific duty imposed on pig-iron; hammered bar was charged with 75 cents a hundred-weight, instead of 45 cents, as in 1816; and higher duties were put on castings, anchors, nails, and spikes. These duties were comparatively heavy; and with a steady fall in the price of iron, especially after the crisis of 1818–19, they became proportionately heavier and heavier. Nevertheless, in the tariff of 1824 they were further increased. The rate on hammered bar went up to 90 cents a hundred-weight; that on rolled bar still remained at $1.50, as it had been fixed in 1816. In 1828 a still further increase was made in the specific duties on all kinds of iron, although the continual fall in prices was of itself steadily increasing the weight of the specific duties. The duty on pig-iron went up to 62½ cents a hundred-weight; that on hammered bar to a cent a pound (that is, $1.12 a hundred-weight); that on rolled bar to $37 a ton. In 1832 duties were reduced in the main to the level of those of 1824, and in 1833 the Compromise Act, after maintaining the duties of 1832 for two years, gradually reduced them still further, till in 1842 they reached a uniform level of 20 per cent. On the whole, it is clear that after 1818 a system of increasingly heavy protection was applied to the iron manufacture, and that for twenty years this protection was maintained without a break. From 1818 till 1837 or 1838, when the reduction of duty under the Compromise Act began to take effect to an appreciable extent, the duties on iron in its various forms ranged from 40 to 100 per cent. on the value.

It is worth while to dwell for a moment on the heavy duty on rolled iron—much higher than that on hammered iron — which was adopted in 1816, and maintained throughout this period. Congress attempted to ward off the competition of the cheaper rolled iron by this heavy discriminating duty, which in 1828 was equivalent to one hundred per cent. on the value. When first established in 1816, the discrimination was defended on the ground that the rolled iron was of inferior quality, and that the importation of the unserviceable article should be impeded for the benefit of the consumer. The scope of the change in the iron manufacture, of which the appearance of rolled iron was one sign, was hardly understood in 1816 and 1818, and this argument against its use may have represented truthfully the animus of the discriminating duty. But in later years the wish to protect the consumer from impositions hardly continued to be the motive for retaining the duty. Rolled bar-iron soon became a well-known article, of considerable importance in commerce. The discriminating duty was retained throughout, and in 1828 even increased; it was still levied in the tariff of 1832; it reappeared when the Whigs carried the tariff of 1842; and it did not finally disappear till 1846. The real motive for maintaining the heavy tax through these years undoubtedly was the unwillingness of the domestic producers to face the competition of the cheaper article. The tax is a clear illustration of that tendency to fetter and impede the progress of improvement which is inherent in protective legislation. It laid a considerable burden on the community, and, as we shall see, it was of no service in encouraging the early growth of the iron industry. It is curious to note that the same contest against improved processes was carried on in France, by a discriminating duty on English rolled iron, levied first in 1816, and not taken off till 1860.

After 1815 the iron-makers of the United States met with strong foreign competition from two directions. In the first place, English pig and rolled iron was being produced with steadily decreasing cost. The use of coke became universal in England, and improvements in methods of production were constantly made. Charcoal continued to be used exclusively in the furnaces of this country; for the possibility of using anthracite had not yet been discovered, and the bituminous coal fields lay too far from what was then the region of dense population to be available. While coke-iron was thus driving out charcoal-iron for all purposes for which the former could be used, the production of charcoal-iron itself encountered the competition of Sweden and Russia. As the United States advanced in population, the more accessible forests became exhausted, and the greater quantity of charcoal-iron needed with the increase of population and of production, could be obtained at home only at higher cost. The Scandinavian countries and Russia, with large forests and a population content with low returns for labor, in large part supplied the increased quantity at lower rates than the iron-makers of this country. Hence the imports of iron show a steady increase, both those of pig-iron and those of rolled and hammered bar; the rolled bar coming from England, and the hammered bar from Sweden and Russia. The demand for iron was increasing at a rapid rate, and there was room for an increase both of the domestic production and of imports; but the rise in imports was marked. Notwithstanding the heavy duties, the proportion of imported to domestic iron from 1818 to 1840 remained about the same.

Since importations continued regularly and on a considerable scale, the price of the iron made at home was clearly raised, at the seaboard, over the price of the foreign iron by the amount of the duty. The country, therefore, paid the iron tax probably on the greater part used, whether of foreign or domestic origin, in the shape of prices from forty to one hundred per cent. higher than those at which the iron could have been bought abroad.

The fact that the manufacture, notwithstanding the heavy and long-continued protection which it enjoyed, was unable to supply the country with the iron which it needed, is of itself sufficient evidence that its protection as a young industry was not successful. It is an essential condition for the usefulness of assistance given to a young industry, that the industry shall ultimately supply its products at least as cheaply as they can be obtained by importation; and this the iron manufacture failed to do. There is, however, more direct evidence than this, that the manufacture was slow to make improvements in production, which might have enabled it eventually to furnish the whole supply needed by the country, and in this way might have justified the heavy taxes laid for its benefit. Pig-iron continued to be made only with charcoal. The process of puddling did not begin to be introduced before 1830, and then inefficiently and on a small scale. Not until the decade between 1830 and 1840, at a time when the Compromise Act of 1833 was steadily decreasing duties, was puddling generally introduced. The iron rails needed for the railroads built at this time — the first parts of the present railroad system — were supplied exclusively by importation. In 1832 an act of Congress had provided that duties should be refunded on all imported rails laid down within three years from the date of importation. Under this act all the first railroads imported their rails without payment of duty. Finally, the great change which put the iron manufacture on a firm and durable basis did not come till the end of the decade 1830–40, when all industry was much depressed, and duties had nearly reached their lowest point. That change consisted in the use of anthracite coal in the blast-furnace. A patent for smelting iron with anthracite was taken out in 1833; the process was first used successfully in 1836. In 1838 and 1839 anthracite began to be widely used. The importance of the discovery was promptly recognized; it was largely adopted in the next decade, and led, among other causes, to the rapid increase of the production of iron, which has been so often ascribed exclusively to the protection of the tariff of 1842. With this change the growth of the iron manufacture on a great scale properly begins.

It seems clear that no connection can be traced between the introduction and early progress of the iron manufacture, and protective legislation. During the colonial period, as we have seen, under the old system of production of iron, the country had exported and not imported iron. The production of charcoal-iron and of hammered bar was carried on before the adoption of the Constitution. During the first twenty years after 1789, the iron-makers still held their own, although the progress of invention elsewhere, and the general tendency in favor of heavy imports, caused a growing importation from abroad. The production of iron by the old methods and with the use of charcoal was therefore in no sense a new industry. If the business of making charcoal-iron could not be carried on or increased during this and the subsequent period, the cause must have lain in natural obstacles and disadvantages which no protection could remove. After 1815, the new

régime in the iron trade had begun; the use of coke in the blast-furnace, and the production of wrought-iron by puddling and rolling, had changed completely the conditions of production. The protective legislation which began in 1818, and continued in force for nearly twenty years, was intended, it is true, to ward off rather than to encourage the adoption of the new methods; but it is conceivable that, contrary to the intentions of its authors, it might have had the latter effect. No such effect, however, is to be seen. During the first ten or fifteen years after the application of protection, no changes of any kind took place. Late in the protective period, and at a time when duties were becoming smaller, the puddling process was introduced. The great change which marks the turning-point in the history of the iron manufacture in the United States — the use of anthracite — began when protection ceased. It is probably not true, as is asserted by advocates of free trade, that protection had any appreciable influence in retarding the use of coal in making iron. Other causes, mainly the refractory nature of the fuel, sufficiently account for the failure to use anthracite at an earlier date. The successful attempts to use anthracite were made almost simultaneously in England and in the United States. The failure to use coke from bituminous coal, which had been employed in England for over half-a-century, was the result of the distance of the bituminous coal-fields from the centre of population, and of the absence of the facility of transportation which has since been given by railroads. It is hardly probable, therefore, that protection exercised any considerable harmful influence in retarding the progress of improvement. But it is clear, on the other hand, that no advantages were obtained from protection in stimulating progress. No change was made during the period of protection which enabled the country to obtain the metal more cheaply than by importation, or even as cheaply. The duties simply taxed the community; they did not serve to stimulate the industry, though they probably did not appreciably retard its growth. We may therefore conclude that the duties on iron during the generation after 1815 formed a heavy tax on consumers; that they impeded, so far as they went, the industrial development of the country; and that no compensatory benefits were obtained to offset these disadvantages.

Concluding Remarks

The three most important branches of industry to which protection has been applied, have now been examined. It has appeared that the introduction of the cotton manufacture took place before the era of protection, and that — looking aside from the anomalous conditions of the period of restriction from 1808 to 1815 — its early progress, though perhaps somewhat promoted by the minimum duty of 1816, would hardly have been much retarded in the absence of protective duties. The manufacture of woollens received little direct assistance before it reached that stage at which it could maintain itself without help, if it were for the advantage of the country that it should be maintained. In the iron manufacture twenty years of heavy protection did not materially alter the proportion of home and foreign supply, and brought about no change in methods of production. It is not possible, and hardly necessary, to carry the inquiry much further. Detailed accounts cannot be obtained of other industries to which protection was applied; but so far as can be seen, the same course of events took place in them as in the three whose history we have followed. The same general conditions affected the man-

ufactures of glass, earthenware, paper, cotton-bagging, sail-duck, cordage, and other articles to which protection was applied during this time with more or less vigor. We may assume that the same general effect, or absence of effect, followed in these as in the other cases. It is not intended to speak of the production of agricultural commodities like sugar, wool, hemp, and flax, to which also protection was applied. In the production of these the natural advantages of one country over another tell more decidedly and surely than in the case of most manufactures, and it has not often been supposed that they come within the scope of the argument we are considering.

Although, therefore, the conditions existed under which it is most likely that protection to young industries may be advantageously applied — a young and undeveloped country in a stage of transition from a purely agricultural to a more diversified industrial condition; this transition, moreover, coinciding in time with great changes in the arts, which made the establishment of new industries peculiarly difficult — notwithstanding the presence of these conditions, little, if any thing, was gained by the protection which the United States maintained in the first part of this century. Two causes account for this. On the one hand, the character of the people rendered the transition of productive forces to manufactures comparatively easy; on the other hand, the shock to economic habits during the restrictive period from 1808 to 1815 effectually prepared the way for such a transition. The genius of the people for mechanical arts showed itself early. Naturally it appeared with most striking results in those fields in which the circumstances of the country gave the richest opportunities; as in the application of steam-power to navigation, in the invention and improvement of tools, and especially of agricultural implements, and in the cotton manufacture. The ingenuity and inventiveness of American mechanics have become traditional, and the names of Whitney and Fulton need only be mentioned to show that these qualities were not lacking at the time we are considering. The presence of such men rendered it more easy to remove the obstacles arising from want of skill and experience in manufactures. The political institutions, the high average of intelligence, the habitual freedom of movement from place to place and from occupation to occupation, also made the rise of the existing system of manufacturing production at once more easy and less dangerous than the same change in other countries. At the same time it so happened that the embargo, the non-intercourse acts, and the war of 1812 rudely shook the country out of the grooves in which it was running, and brought about a state of confusion from which the new industrial system could emerge more easily than from a well-settled organization of industry. The restrictive period may indeed be considered to have been one of extreme protection. The stimulus which it gave to some manufactures perhaps shows that the first steps in these were not taken without some artificial help. The intrinsic soundness of the argument for protection to young industries therefore may not be touched by the conclusions drawn from the history of its trial in the United States, which shows only that the intentional protection of the tariffs of 1816, 1824, and 1828 had little effect. The period from 1808 till the financial crisis of 1818–19 was a disturbed and chaotic one, from which the country settled down, with little assistance from protective legislation, into a new arrangement of its productive forces.

Suggestions for Additional Reading

More words were printed in the United States on the subject of the tariff during the eighteen twenties and early thirties than on any other public question. Only a specialist on the period can hope to read more than a small fraction of this material. However, so much of what was written was repetition that by careful sampling the student can obtain a fairly reliable picture. Most useful are the debates in Congress on the numerous tariff bills which were introduced during the period. The House of Representatives was the great popular forum of the period and the debates of that body, reproduced and discussed across the land in newspapers, in magazines, and in pamphlet form became a universal subject for editorials, sermons, and village store disputes. The congressional speeches are to be found up to 1824 in the *Annals of the Congress of the United States* and thereafter to 1837 in *Register of Debates in Congress*. Both of these many-volumed works contain numerous memorials submitted on the subject by interested groups.

For the periodical literature of the time *Niles' Weekly Register*, published throughout the period, best represents the protectionist view. This may well be supplemented by sampling the many books and pamphlets written and published by Mathew Carey. Many newspapers and periodicals, especially those published in the South, present the free trade viewpoint but none, perhaps, is more valuable than that of Condy Raguet. His journal, begun as the *Free Trade*

Advocate in 1829, soon became the *Banner of the Constitution,* lasting in this form until the end of 1832, when, after an interval, it continued for a short time as *The Examiner.*

Writings of contemporary economists, in addition to those of Daniel Raymond and Thomas R. Dew, which are included in this volume, are also worth some attention. Best for the protectionist viewpoint are Friedrich List, *Outlines of American Political Economy* (Philadelphia, 1827), and Willard Phillips, *A Manual of Political Economy* (Boston, 1828). Among the economists attacking protectionism, the student may well examine for the Southern viewpoint Thomas Cooper, *Lectures on the Elements of Political Economy* (Columbia, S. C., 1826), and for the Northern view John McVickar, *Outlines of Political Economy* (New York, 1825). The latter is a republication of an article by the British economist John R. McCulloch, with notes by McVickar. It is sometimes cited under McCulloch's name.

Like the contemporary material, most of the historical writing on the period covered by this volume is definitely pro- or anti-tariff. From the former viewpoint the most substantial study is Edward Stanwood, *American Tariff Controversies in the Nineteenth Century* (Boston, 1904), Vol. I. This largely nonanalytical work emphasizes political aspects and is made up in considerable part of excerpts from current speeches and documents. Other protectionist works which give appreciable attention to the history of the period covered by this volume are highly partisan accounts similar to the excerpt included from the book by D. G. Harriman. Typical examples of such appraisals will be found in Frederic E. Kip, *The Democratic Underwood-Simmons Tariff Bill: A Colossal Failure and Most Disastrous to Labor, Industry and Agriculture, As Has Been All Legislation for Tariff for Revenue Only, from 1789 to 1913* (Montclair, New Jersey, no date); and William McKinley, *The Tariff, A Review of the Tariff Legislation of the United States from 1812 to 1896* (New York, 1904). The economists who have written on United States tariff history have been generally critical of protection. Here the standard work is, of course, F. W. Taussig, *The Tariff History of the United States,* which has appeared in many editions. In addition to the material from Taussig included in this volume, the student will benefit from reading the essays in Taussig's *Tariff History* entitled, "The Early Protective Movement and the Tariff of 1828" and "The Tariff, 1830–1860."

Doctrinal aspects of the controversy are well digested in Joseph Dorfman, *The Economic Mind in American Civilization,* *1606–1865* (New York, 1946), and Carl William Kaiser, Jr., *History of the Academic Protectionist–Free Trade Controversy in America Before 1860* (Philadelphia, 1939). The situation in an important state is analyzed in Malcolm Rogers Eiselen, *The Rise of Pennsylvania Protectionism* (Philadelphia, 1932). Brief expositions of tariff history will also be found in the standard texts in economic history. See, for example, Harold Underwood Faulkner, *American Economic History* (New York, 1949); Edward C. Kirkland, *A History of American Economic Life* (New York, 1951); and Chester W. Wright, *Economic History of the United States* (New York, 1941). Also useful are special studies, such as Victor S. Clark, *History of Manufactures in the United States* (Vol. I., New York, 1929), and Chester W. Wright, *Wool-Growing and the Tariff, A Study in the Economic History of the United States* (Boston, 1910). Not to be overlooked is the excellent brief analysis by Guy Stevens Callender, *Selections from the Economic History of the United States, 1765–1860* (Boston, 1909) pp. 487–490.